POCKET

BANGKOK

TOP SIGHTS • LOCAL EXPERIENCES

AUSTIN BUSH

Contents

Plan Your Trip

Wat Arun (p40)
ARINCHAWIT JIT/SHUTTERSTOCK ©

Explore Bangkok 29

Worth a Trip

Survival Guide 169

Special Features

Welcome to Bangkok

For decades, Bangkok was seen as little more than a necessary stop-over before hitting the islands. But the Bangkok of today is a destination. What other city has such a no-holds-barred approach to eating? Bangkok's older districts retain the grit, charm and character of the past.

Temple housing the Emerald Buddha, Wat Phra Kaew (p32)
MIKI STUDIO/SHUTTERSTOCK ©

Top Sights

Jim Thompson House

Bangkok's most famous residence. **p96**

Chatuchak Weekend Market

The city's most impressive market.
p160

Wat Phra Kaew & Grand Palace

A sacred enclave.
p32

Wat Arun

The capital's most famous riverside temple. **p40**

Wat Traimit

Visit the golden Buddha. **p78**

Ayuthaya

Day trip to ancient Thailand. **p166**

Dusit Palace Park
Bangkok's fairy-tale palace. **p74**

Ko Kret
Bangkok's island getaway. **p164**

Wat Pho
Bangkok's biggest reclining Buddha. **p36**

Eating

Nowhere else is the Thai reverence for food more evident than in Bangkok. To the outsider, the life of a Bangkokian appears to be a string of meals and snacks punctuated by the odd stab at work, not the other way around. If you can adjust your mental clock to this schedule, your visit will be a delicious one indeed.

Street Food

Open-air markets and food stalls are among the most popular dining spots for Thais. In the mornings, stalls selling coffee and Chinese-style doughnuts spring up along busy commuter corridors. At lunchtime, diners might grab a plastic chair at yet another stall for a simple stir-fry. In Bangkok's suburbs, night markets often set up in the middle of town with a cluster of food vendors, metal tables and chairs.

Fine Dining

Most people associate Bangkok exclusively with street food, but the city's eating scene is increasingly diverse. The fine-dining establishments range in cuisine from French to Thai, including several forays into fusion. Best of all, this is Bangkok, so there's little of the stuffiness associated with fine dining in the West.

Ethnic Cuisines

Contemporary Bangkok's menu extends far beyond Thai;

reconsider rice for a meal or two and jump head first into a dining scene where options range from Korean to Egyptian, touching on just about everything in between.

Best Street Food

Jay Fai Some of the most legendary – and expensive – noodles in town. (p63)

Pa Aew Stall specialising in Bangkok-style fare. (p49)

Thanon Phadungdao Seafood Stalls These stalls are so 'street' you risk getting bumped by a car. (p89)

Khun Yah Cuisine The flavours of Bangkok and central Thailand in one convenient location. (p87)

DESIGN PICS/RAY LASKOWITZ/GETTY IMAGES ©

Best Fine Dining

nahm Widely considered to be Southeast Asia's best restaurant. (p125)

Eat Me Eclectic, eccentric modern cuisine, paired with great service. (p125)

Appia Sublime yet homey Italian. (p147)

Sra Bua by Kiin Kiin A modern, innovative venue where Thai flavours, ingredients and presentation are taken to the next level. (p107)

Le Normandie Dress up for an upmarket and old-world 'Continental' dining experience. (p129)

Best Ethnic Cuisines

Jidori Cuisine Ken Perfect Japanese-style chicken skewers. (p147)

Tonkin-Annam Some of the best Vietnamese food in Bangkok. (p49)

Fou de Joie French in a retro setting. (p87)

Shoshana This backpacker staple has been proffering the flavours of Jerusalem

for more than 30 years now. (p63)

Din Tai Fung Famed Taiwanese chain that is *the* place to go for *xiao long bao*, Chinese 'soup' dumplings. (p104)

Chennai Kitchen Bangkok's best southern Indian cuisine. (p128)

Nasir Al-Masri Authentic Middle Eastern in the heart of Bangkok's Middle Eastern hood. (p149)

Foodie Websites

Keep with the ever-changing food scene in Bangkok by following the Restaurants section of **BK** (bk.asia-city.com/restaurants) or **Bangkok 101** (www.bangkok101.com).

Shopping

Prime your credit card and shine your baht: shopping is serious business in Bangkok. Hardly a street corner in the city is free from a vendor, hawker or impromptu stall. It doesn't stop there: Bangkok is also home to one of the world's largest outdoor markets, not to mention Southeast Asia's second-largest mall.

Malls & Markets

Although the tourist brochures tend to tout the upmarket malls, Bangkok still lags slightly behind Singapore and Hong Kong in this area. The open-air markets are where the best deals and most original items are found.

Bargaining

At Bangkok's markets and at some of its malls, you'll have to bargain for most, if not all, items. In general, if you see a price tag, it means that the price is fixed and bargaining isn't an option.

Gems & Jewellery

Countless tourists are sucked into gem scams in which they are taken to a shop by a helpful stranger and tricked into buying bulk gems that can supposedly be resold in their home country for 100% profit. The expert con artists seem trustworthy and convince tourists that they need a citizen's help to circumvent tricky customs regulations. Unsurprisingly, the gem world doesn't work like that, and what most tourists end up with are worthless pieces of glass.

Best Markets

Chatuchak Weekend Market One of the world's largest markets and a must-do Bangkok experience. (p160)

Thanon Khao San Market Elephant-print pants, Singha shirts, fresh-squeezed orange juice; all the backpacker essentials are available here. (p72)

Pak Khlong Talat Bangkok's famous flower market; come late at night and don't forget your camera. (p85)

Talat Mai This frenetic fresh market is a slice of China in Bangkok. (p84)

NENG TIEO/SHUTTERSTOCK ©

Best for Traditional Souvenirs

Heritage Craft Unique goods from just about every corner of the country. (p72)

Lofty Bamboo Hill-tribe inspired clothes and handicrafts. (p73)

Tamnan Mingmuang Classy items woven from rattan and water hyacinth. (p136)

Best for Quirky Souvenirs

The Selected A carefully curated assemblage of modern, mostly Thai-made housewares, knick-knacks, clothing and accessories. (p110)

Mowaan Lozenges, inhalers, oils and balms rooted in Thai herbal medicine. (p72)

it's going green Retro Thai-style homewares, soaps and other items that double as one-of-a-kind souvenirs. (p110)

Objects of Desire Store Design-focused contemporary ceramics, paper products, furniture and other homewares. (p110)

Chiang Heng Third-generation family-run kitchen-supply shop. (p136)

Best Malls

Siam Discovery Recently renovated, this is hands down the most design-conscious mall in town. (p111)

MBK Center A seemingly never-ending Thai market in a mall. (p111)

Siam Center The third floor here is one of the best locations to check out established local labels. (p112)

Insider Online Shopping Tips

Nancy Chandler's Map of Bangkok (www.nancychandler.net) is a colourful online guide that highlights the quirkier types of shopping venues, which you won't find included on free tourist maps.

Drinking & Nightlife

Shame on you if you think Bangkok's only nightlife options include the word 'go-go'. As in any big international city, the drinking and partying scene in Bangkok ranges from trashy to classy and touches on just about everything in between.

Cocktails

Blue kamikazes no longer cut it in Bangkok; today the city is home to a growing repertoire of bars that take pride in mixing the classics or inventing new drinks altogether.

Beer

The domestic brews still corner most of the market, but labels from around the world have found their way to Bangkok (although they don't come cheap).

Rooftop Bars

Bangkok is one of the few big cities in the world where nobody seems to mind if you slap the odd bar or restaurant on top of a skyscraper. The options range from cheap to chic to and, likewise, range in view from hyperurban to suburban.

Live Music

Music is an essential element of a Thai night out, and just about every pub worth its salted peanuts has a house band.

Clubs

Clubs in Bangkok tend to heave on certain nights – Fridays and Saturdays, during a visit from a foreign DJ, or for a night dedicated to the music flavour of the month – then hibernate every other night.

Best for Cocktails

WTF The classics – done well. (p150)

Q&A Bar Sophisticated mixed drinks in a venue with a midcentury vibe. (p150)

Ku Bar Edgy cocktails in an even edgier locale. (p68)

SHANTI HESSE/SHUTTERSTOCK ©

Best Rooftop Bars

Moon Bar The combination of casual ambience and stunning views make this our personal favourite of Bangkok's original rooftop bars. (p130)

River Vibe Budget guesthouse prices, million-dollar views. (p91)

Sky Bar The sweeping Hollywood entrance and seemingly floating bar set the tone at this rooftop venue. (p139)

Best Clubs

Beam At press time, Bangkok's best nightclub. (p153)

Glow Club with underground cred. (p155)

Demo Where Bangkok's young and beautiful go. (p155)

The Club Dance with a virtual UN of partiers at this Th Khao San–based disco. (p68)

Best Live Music

Titanium Nightly performances by Unicorn, an all-girl band that's bound to get you bouncing. (p156)

Brick Bar Live-music den, famous among locals, for whom dancing on the tables is practically mandatory. (p70)

Best for Beer

Hair of the Dog A fridge full of bottles from around the world and 13 taps. (p108)

Pijiu Bar Craft brews and Chinatown-influenced charcuterie platters. (p90)

Mikkeller Some of the city's most unique micro- and craft-brews. (p152)

The Living Room As the name suggests, live jazz in a comfortable setting. (p155)

Guides to Bangkok's Nightlife

To find out what's on when you're in town, go to **BK** (bk.asia-city.com), **Bangkok 101** (www.bangkok101.com), the Bangkok Post's Friday supplement, *Guru*, or **Siam-2nite** (www.siam2nite.com)

Temples

IPHOTO-THAILAND/SHUTTERSTOCK ©

A Thai temple (wát) is a compound of different buildings serving specific religious functions. Even if you don't consider yourself spiritual, Bangkok's wát provide pleasures that range in scope from artistic inspiration to urban exploration.

Thai Architecture

Considered the highest art form in Thai society, traditional Thai temple architecture follows relatively strict rules of design that dictate proportion, placement, materials and ornamentation. In addition to the native Siamese styles of building, within Bangkok's temples you'll also find examples from historical Khmer, Mon, Lao and northern Thai traditions.

Buddha Images

Every wát in Bangkok has a Buddha image, which for the most part is sculpted according to strict iconographical rules found in Buddhist art texts dating to the 3rd century AD. There are four basic postures and positions: standing, sitting, walking and reclining.

Best Temples

Wat Pho If you haven't seen the ginormous reclining Buddha here, you haven't seen Bangkok. (p43)

Wat Phra Kaew The granddaddy of Bangkok temples and the home of a certain Emerald Buddha. (p43)

Wat Suthat Home to one of Thailand's biggest Buddhas and equally impressive floor-to-ceiling temple murals. (p58)

Wat Traimit Residence of the world's largest golden Buddha. (p78)

Wat Arun This predecessor to Bangkok is also one of the few Thai temples you're allowed to partially climb on. (p43)

Golden Mount & Wat Saket Hilltop temple with great views over old Bangkok. (p58)

Wat Mangkon Kamalawat The epitome of the hectic, smoky, noisy Chinese-style temple. (p84)

Cooking Classes

Consuming everything Bangkok has to offer is one thing, but imagine the points you'll rack up if you can make the same dishes for your friends back home. A visit to a Thai cooking school has become a must-do on many Bangkok itineraries; for some visitors it is a highlight of their trip.

AUSTIN BUSH/LONELY PLANET ©

Best Cooking Classes

Amita Thai Cooking Class (📞02 466 8966; www.amitathaicooking. com; 162/17 Soi 14, Th Wutthakat, Thonburi; classes 3000B; ⏰9.30am-1pm Thu-Tue; 🚤klorng boat from Maharaj Pier) One of Bangkok's most charming cooking schools is held in this canalside house in Thonburi.

Cooking with Poo & Friends (📞080 434 8686; www.cookingwith poo.com; classes 1500B; ⏰8.30am-1pm; 👪) Popular course established by a Bangkok native. (p147)

Bangkok Bold Cooking Studio (📞098 829 4310; www.facebook.com/ bangkokboldcookingstudio; 503 Th Phra Sumen; classes 2500-4500B; ⏰11am-2pm; 🚤klorng boat to Phanfa Leelard Pier) Daily courses ranging in difficulty from beginner to intermediate in three Thai dishes, with lessons taught in a chic shophouse setting.

Silom Thai Cooking School (📞084 726 5669; www.bangkokthaicooking. com; 68 Soi 13, Th Silom; classes from 900B; ⏰9am-12.20pm, 1.40-5pm & 6-9pm; S Chong Nonsi exit 3) The facilities are basic but Silom crams a visit to a local market and instruction of six dishes into four hours, making it the best bang for your baht.

Blue Elephant Thai Cooking School (📞02 673 9353; www.blueele phantcookingschool. com; 233 Th Sathon Tai/ South; classes from 3295B; ⏰8.45am-1pm & 1.30-4.30pm Mon-Sat; S Surasak exit 2) Bangkok's most chichi Thai cooking school offers two lessons daily. The morning class has a market visit, while the afternoon session includes a detailed introduction to Thai ingredients.

Massage & Spa

AKAPHON/SHUTTERSTOCK ©

Bangkok could mount a strong claim to being the massage capital of the world. According to the teachings of traditional Thai healing, the use of herbs and massage should be part of a regular health-and-beauty regimen, not just an excuse for pampering – music to the ears of many a visitor to Bangkok.

Best Thai Massage

Health Land (☎02 637 8883; www.healthlandspa.com; 120 Th Sathon Neua/North; 2hr massage 550B; ◷9am-11pm; Ⓢ Surasak exit 3) Astoundingly good-value, traditional Thai massage in a clean, contemporary setting.

Asia Herb Association (☎02 392 3631; www.asiaherbassociation.com; 58/19-25 Soi 55/Thong Lor, Th Sukhumvit; Thai massage 1hr 500B, with herbal compress 1½hr 1100B; ◷9am-midnight; Ⓢ Thong Lo exit 3) Massage with an emphasis on Thai-style herbal compresses.

Ruen-Nuad Massage Studio (☎02 632 2662; 42 Th Convent; massage per hour 350B; ◷10am-9pm; Ⓜ Si Lom exit 2, Ⓢ Sala Daeng exit 2) Charming house-bound massage studio.

Best Spas

Oriental Spa (☎02 659 9000; www.mandarinoriental.com; Mandarin Oriental, 48 Soi 40/Oriental, Th Charoen Krung; massage & spa packages from 2900B; ◷9am-10pm; ⛴Oriental Pier or hotel shuttle boat from Sathon/Central Pier) One of Bangkok's – and Asia's – most lauded spas, although it doesn't come cheap.

Spa 1930 (☎02 254 8606; www.spa1930.com; 42 Th Ton Son; Thai massage from 1000B, spa packages from 3500B; ◷9.30am-9.30pm; Ⓢ Chit Lom exit 4) Cosy spa located in an antique house.

Thann Sanctuary (☎02 658 6557; www.thannsanctuaryspa.info; 2nd fl, CentralWorld, Th Ratchadamri; Thai massage from 2000B, spa treatments from 2800B; ◷10am-9pm; Ⓢ Chit Lom exit 9 to Sky Walk, Siam exit 6 to Sky Walk) Chic mall-bound spa employing the eponymous brand's fragrant herbal products.

For Kids

KOKTARO/SHUTTERSTOCK ©

There isn't a whole lot of attractions in Bangkok meant to appeal directly to the little ones, but there's no lack of locals willing to provide attention. This means kids are welcome almost anywhere and you'll rarely experience the sort of eye-rolling annoyance that can occur in the West.

Infants

Nappies (diapers), international brands of milk formula and other infant requirements are widely available. For moving by foot, slings are often more useful than prams, as Bangkok footpaths are infamously uneven.

Eating with Kids

Dining with children in Thailand, particularly with infants, is a liberating experience. Take it for granted that your kids will be fawned over, played with and, more often than not, carried around by restaurant waitstaff.

It's worth noting that high chairs are rarely found, except at expensive restaurants.

Best for Kids

KidZania (☎ 02 683 1888; www.bangkok.kidzania.com; 5th fl, Siam Paragon, 991/1 Rama I; adult 425-500B, child 425-1000B; ⊙10am-5pm Mon-Fri, 10.30am-8pm Sat & Sun; Ⓢ Siam exits 3 & 5) Vast and modern 'edutainment' complex.

Lumphini Park (สวนลุมพินี; bounded by Th Sarasin, Rama IV, Th Witthayu/Wireless Rd & Th Ratchadamri; ⊙4.30am-9pm; ♿; Ⓜ Lumphini exit 3, Si Lom exit 1, Ⓢ Sala Daeng exit 3, Ratchadamri exit 2) Come here for kite flying (in season February to April), boating and fish feeding.

Queen Saovabha Memorial Institute (สถานเสาวภา, cnr Rama IV & Th Henri Dunant; adult/child 200/50B; ⊙9.30am-3.30pm Mon-Fri, to 1pm Sat & Sun; ♿; Ⓜ Si Lom exit 1, Ⓢ Sala Daeng exit 3) Antivenom-producing snake farm. (p102)

Museum of Siam (สถาบันพิพิธภัณฑ์การเรียนรู้แห่งชาติ; www.museumsiam.org; Th Maha Rat; 300B; ⊙10am-6pm Tue-Sun; ♿; ⛴ Tien Pier) Lots of interactive exhibits that will appeal to kids.

Stanley MiniVenture (www.stanleyminiventure.com; 2nd fl, Gateway Ekamai, 982/22 Th Sukhumvit; adult/child 500/400B; ⊙10am-8pm) A town in miniature.

Tours

JELLY_CHANONKIJ/SHUTTERSTOCK ©

Bangkok is a big, intimidating place and some visitors might appreciate a bit of hand-holding in the form of a guided tour. But even if you already know your way around, themed tours led by a private guide or bicycle tours are great ways to see another side of the city.

Best Tours

Bangkok Food Tours (✆095 943 9222; www.bangkokfoodtours.com; tours from 1150B) Culinary wanders around old Bangkok.

Co van Kessel Bangkok Tours (✆02 639 7351; www.covankessel.com; ground fl, River City, 23 Th Yotha; tours from 950B; ⊙6am-7pm; ⛴River City Pier) Themed bicycle and walking tours of the city.

Pandan Tour (✆02 689 1232, 087 109 8873; www.thaicanaltour.com; tours from 2395B) Small-boat tours of Bangkok's canals.

ABC Amazing Bangkok Cyclists (✆081 812 9641; www.realasia.net; 10/5-7 Soi Aree, Soi 26, Th Sukhumvit; tours from 1300B; ⊙daily tours at 8am, 10am, 1pm & 6pm; ⛹; ⓈPhrom Phong exit 4) Long-running operation with morning, afternoon and all-day bike tours of Bangkok and its suburbs.

Tour with Tong (✆081 835 0240; tours from 1000B) Recommended guides offering private tours in and around Bangkok.

Chili Paste Tours (✆085 143 6779, 094 552 2361; www.foodtoursbangkok.com; tours from 2000B) Culinary tours of Bangkok's older neighbourhoods.

Thai Private Tour Guide (✆082 799 1099; www.thaitourguide.com; tours from 2000B) The guides at this outfit get positive feedback.

Velo Thailand (✆02 628 8628, 089 201 7782; www.velothailand.com; 29 Soi 4, Th Samsen; tours from 1000B; ⊙10am-7pm; ⛴Phra Athit/Banglamphu Pier) Day and night bicycle tours to Thonburi and further afield.

LGBT

Bangkok has a notoriously pink vibe to it. From kinky male underwear shops mushrooming at street corners to lesbian-only get-togethers, one could eat, shop and play here for days without ever leaving the comfort of gay-friendly venues.

ALEXANDER_H_SCHULZ/GETTY IMAGES ©

Lesbians

Lesbians have become much more open and visible in Bangkok in recent years. It's worth noting that, perhaps because Thailand is still a relatively conservative place, lesbians in Bangkok generally adhere to rather strict gender roles. Overtly 'butch' lesbians, called *tom* (from 'tomboy'), typically have short hair, bind their breasts and wear men's clothing. Femme lesbians refer to themselves as *dêe* (from 'lady').

Transgender People

Bangkok is famous for its open and visible transgender population – known locally as *gà·teu·i* (also spelt *kàthoey*). Some are cross-dressers, while others have had sexual-reassignment surgery – Thailand is one of the leading countries for this procedure. *Gà·teu·i* cabarets aimed at tourists are wildly popular.

Best for LGBT Travellers

DJ Station One of the most legendary gay dance clubs in Asia. (p119)

Telephone Pub Longstanding and perpetually buzzy pub, right in the middle of Bangkok's pinkest zone. (p119)

Maggie Choo's Sunday is gay day at this otherwise hetero boozer. (p131)

The Stranger Unapologetically camp transgender stage shows. (p119)

Four Perfect Days

Day 1

CHANTAL DE BRUIJNE/SHUTTERSTOCK ©

Get up as early as you can to take the Chao Phraya Express Boat to Tha Chang to explore Ko Ratanakosin's must-see temples: **Wat Phra Kaew & Grand Palace** (p43), **Wat Pho** (p43) and **Wat Arun** (p43). For lunch, exploreThai flavours at **Err** (p49).

Cross to the Silom area and refresh with a spa treatment at **Health Land** (p122), or soothe those overworked legs at **Ruen-Nuad Massage Studio** (p122). Afterwards, get a new perspective on Bangkok with a rooftop cocktail at **Moon Bar** (p130).

For dinner, **nahm** (p125) serves what is arguably some of the best Thai food in Bangkok. If you've still got it in you, hit **DJ Station** (p119) or any of the other bars and clubs in Bangkok's gaybourhood (p118).

Day 2

COWARDLION/SHUTTERSTOCK ©

Take the BTS (Skytrain) to National Stadium and start your day with a visit to the popular and worthwhile **Jim Thompson House** (p96). Afterwards, check out the latest exhibition at the **Bangkok Art & Culture Centre** (p100).

Next door, **MBK Food Island** (p103) is the ideal introduction to Thai food. After eating, walk through Bangkok's ultra-modern commercial district, stopping off at linked shopping centres **MBK Center** (p111), **Siam Center** (p112) and **Siam Square** (p111). Be sure to throw in a prayer for good luck at the **Erawan Shrine** (p102).

Dine on refined Thai dishes at **Saneh Jaan** (p104). If it's a weekday or Sunday, consider catching a Thai-boxing match at **Rajadamnern Stadium** (p70).

Day 3

AUSTIN BUSH/LONELY PLANET ©

Combine canals and the culinary arts at **Amita Thai Cooking Class** (p17). Cross the river and spend the afternoon visiting the **Golden Mount** (p58), **Wat Suthat** (p58), the artisan village **Ban Baat** (p60), or the bizarre strip of religious commerce that is **Thanon Bamrung Meuang** (p72). Spend the afternoon in the famous backpacker melting pot of Th Khao San (p61), people-watching and picking up souvenirs at **Thanon Khao San Market** (p72).

For dinner, head to Th Sukhumvit and take a temporary break from Thai food at one of this strip's great international restaurants, such as **Jidori Cuisine Ken** (p147). End your night with a Thai-themed cocktail at a cosy local, such as **WTF** (p150), or extend the night with a visit to a club like **Beam** (p153).

Day 4

VASSAMON ANANSUKKASEM/SHUTTERSTOCK ©

If it's a weekend, consider a half day of shopping at the **Chatuchak Weekend Market** (p160), which also has a seemingly endless stream of cheap and tasty food stalls. Otherwise, take a half day excursion outside the city to the artificial island of **Ko Kret** (p164), or a day trip to **Ayuthaya** (p166).

Take time to recover from the market (or your excursion). In the relative cool of the late afternoon take the MRT (metro) to Chinatown and visit the home of the Golden Buddha, **Wat Traimit** (p78). Follow our walking tour of Chinatown's best street eats (p80).

Cross to Banglamphu and begin the evening with sophisticated cocktails at **Ku Bar** (p68), followed by a rowdy live-music show at **Brick Bar** (p70).

Need to Know

For detailed information, see Survival Guide (p169)

Language
Thai

Currency
Thai baht (B)

Visas
Most international air arrivals are eligible for a 30-day visa exemption; 60-day visas are available from a Thai consulate before leaving home.

Money
Most places deal only with cash. ATMs are widespread but charge a 200B foreign-transaction fee. Some foreign credit and debit cards are accepted in high-end hotels, resturants and shops.

Mobile Phones
GSM and 4G networks available through inexpensive SIM cards.

Time
Bangkok (GMT/UTC plus seven hours)

Tipping
Tipping is generally not expected in Thailand.

Daily Budget

Budget: Less than 1500B
Dorm bed/basic guesthouse room: 150–800B
Street-stall meals: 150–300B
One or two of the big-hitter sights: 500–600B
Getting around on public transport: 20–100B

Midrange: 1500–4000B
Flashpacker guesthouse or midrange hotel room: 800–1500B
Street and restaurant meals: 500–1000B
Most, if not all, of the big sights: 500–1000B
Getting around with public transport and occasional taxis: 100–300B

Top end: More than 4000B
Boutique hotel room: 4000B
Fine dining: 1500–3000B
Private tours from: 1000B
Getting around in taxis: 300–800B

Advance Planning

Three months before Book a room at a smaller boutique hotel, especially if visiting during December/January.

One month before Make reservations at the critically acclaimed nahm (p125) restaurant; if you plan to stay in Thailand longer than 30 days, apply for a visa at the Thai embassy or consulate in your home country.

One week before Book lessons at a Thai cooking school.

Arriving in Bangkok

Most travellers will arrive in Bangkok via air.

✈ Suvarnabhumi International Airport

Around 30 minutes east of Central Bangkok.

Train Airport Rail Link connects Phaya Thai station with Suvarnabhumi, 6am to 12am, 45B

Bus Suvarnabhumi to Th Khao San, 6am to 8pm, 60B

Meter taxis 24hr, 200B–300B plus a 50B airport surcharge and optional expressway tolls

✈ Don Mueang International Airport

Around one hour north of Central Bangkok.

Bus every 30 minutes 7.30am to 11.30pm, 50B

Meter taxis 24hr, starting at approximately 200B plus a 50B airport surcharge

Getting Around

Bangkok's transport system is improving and, although you'll probably find yourself stuck in traffic at some point, the jams aren't as epic as they used to be.

🚃 BTS

The elevated Skytrain runs from 6am to midnight. Tickets 16B to 44B.

🚃 MRT

The Metro runs from 6am to midnight. Tickets 16B to 42B.

🚗 Taxi

Outside of rush hours, Bangkok taxis are a great bargain. Flagfall 35B.

🚢 Chao Phraya Express Boat

Runs 6am to 8pm, charging 10B to 40B.

🚢 Klorng Boat

Bangkok's canal boats run from 5.30am to 8pm most days. Tickets 9B to 19B.

🚌 Bus

Cheap, but a slow and confusing way to get around Bangkok. Tickets 5B to 30B.

Bangkok Neighbourhoods

Banglamphu (p53)
Despite the presence of Th Khao San, Banglamphu is classic 'Bangkok' with its antique shophouses and temples.

Ko Ratanakosin & Thonburi (p31)
Bangkok's riverside historical centre includes monuments to king, country and religion that draw most tourists.

Dusit Palace
Park

Wat Phra Kaew & Grand Palace

Wat Pho

Wat Arun

Wat Traimit

Chinatown (p77)
Chinatown is Bangkok's most hectic neighbourhood with shark-fin restaurants, gaudy gold and flashing neon signs.

⊙ Chatuchak Weekend Market

Siam Square, Pratunam, Phloen Chit & Ratchathewi (p95)

The area around Siam Square is essentially one giant shopping mall, and today is considered the unofficial centre of modern Bangkok.

Thanon Sukhumvit (p141)

East of central Bangkok is Sukhumvit, a busy commercial and residential area that's a favourite with both expatriates and locals.

⊙ Jim Thompson House

Riverside, Silom & Lumphini (p117)

This is Bangkok's defacto financial district, and most locals come here to work, while you'll probably come to eat, play or stay.

Explore
Bangkok

Dancers, Erawan Shrine (p102) BOGOSHIPDA/SHUTTERSTOCK ©

Explore ⊕
Ko Ratanakosin
& Thonburi

The artificial island of Ko Ratanakosin is the birthplace of Bangkok and packed full of sights. If you've come for the sights, arrive early, while the heat is still tolerable and the touts few. Evening is best for photography, particularly if you're hoping for the classic sunset shot of Wat Arun. By contrast, Thonburi, located across Mae Nam Chao Phraya (Chao Phraya River), is a seemingly forgotten yet visit-worthy zone of sleepy residential districts connected by klorng (canals).

Don't miss Wat Phra Kaew & Grand Palace (p32) then marvel at Wat Pho's immense reclining Buddha (p37). If intellectual stimulation is your thing, investigate exhibits at the Museum of Siam (p45). Come late afternoon, cross the river and visit Wat Arun (p40). Coordinate your return to Ko Ratanakosin with sunset cocktails at Roof (p51) before dinner at a riverside restaurant such as Sala Rattanakosin Eatery & Bar (p51).

Getting There & Around

Ko Ratanakosin is probably Bangkok's most touristy neighbourhood, but hop on any of the 3B river-crossing ferries and you'll be whisked to Thonburi, where regular Thai life carries on uninterrupted.

🚢 **Chao Phraya Express Boat** To Ko Ratanakosin: Tien Pier, Chang Pier, Maharaj Pier and Phra Chan Tai Pier. To Thonburi: Wang Lang/Siriraj Pier, Thonburi Railway Station Pier and Phra Pin Klao Bridge Pier.

S **BTS (Skytrain)** To Ko Ratanakosin: National Stadium or Phaya Thai. To Thonburi: Krung Thonburi and Wongwian Yai.

Neighbourhood Map on p44

Wat Phra Kaew and Grand Palace (p32) TRAVEL MANIA/SHUTTERSTOCK ©

Top Sight 🛕

Wat Phra Kaew & Grand Palace

Also known as the Temple of the Emerald Buddha, Wat Phra Kaew is the colloquial name of the vast fairy-tale-like compound that also includes the Grand Palace, the former residence of the Thai monarch. The ground was consecrated in 1782, the first year of Bangkok rule, and is today Bangkok's biggest tourist attraction and a pilgrimage destination for devout Buddhists and nationalists.

 MAP P44, C4

วัดพระแก้ว, พระบรมมหาราชวัง

Th Na Phra Lan

admission 500B

🕐 8.30am-3.30pm

🚤 Chang Pier, Maharaj Pier, Phra Chan Tai Pier

The Emerald Buddha

On a tall platform in Wat Phra Kaew's fantastically decorated *bòht* (ordination hall), the Emerald Buddha is the temple's primary attraction. The spectacular ornamentation inside and out does an excellent job of distracting first-time visitors from paying their respects to the image. Here's why: the Emerald Buddha is only 66cm tall and sits so high above worshippers in the main temple building that the gilded shrine is more striking than the small figure it cradles. Despite the name, the statue is actually carved from a single piece of nephrite (a type of jade).

No one knows exactly where it came from or who sculpted it, but it first appeared on record in 15th-century Chiang Rai in northern Thailand. Stylistically it seems to belong to Thai artistic periods of the 13th to 14th centuries.

The *bòht* itself is a notable example of the Ratanakosin school of architecture, which combines stylistic holdovers from Ayuthaya along with modern touches from China and the West.

Ramakian Murals

Recently restored murals of the *Ramakian* (the Thai version of the Indian epic *Ramayana*) line the inside walls of the Wat Phra Kaew compound. Originally painted during the reign of Rama I (King Phraphutthayotfa Chulalok; r 1782–1809), the 178 sections, beginning at the north gate and moving clockwise around the compound, describe the struggles of the hero Rama to rescue his kidnapped wife, Sita.

The Guardians of Wat Phra Kaew

The first sights you'll see upon entering Wat Phra Kaew are two 5m-high *yaksha* (giants or ogres; pictured left) with origins in Hindu/Buddhist mythology. Other mythical creatures in the temple compound include the half-human, half-bird *kinnaree* and the sacred birds known as *garuda,* as well as various hermits and elephants.

★ Top Tips

o Enter the complex through the clearly marked third gate from the river pier. Tickets are purchased inside the complex; anyone telling you it's closed is a gem tout or a con artist.

o At Wat Phra Kaew and the Grand Palace grounds, dress rules are strictly enforced. If you're flashing a bit too much skin, expect to be shown into a dressing room and issued with a shirt or sarong (rental is free, but you must provide a refundable 200B deposit).

o Admission to the complex includes entrance to Dusit Palace Park.

✗ Take a Break

Cap off your visit to with lunch at Ming Lee (p50), a charmingly old-school Thai restaurant located virtually across the street from the complex's main entrance. Alternatively, enjoy a Thai-themed cocktail and a spicy drinking snack at Err (p49).

Phra Mondop

Commissioned by Rama I, this structure was built for the storage of sacred Buddhist manuscripts. The seven-tiered roof, floor woven from strands of silver, and intricate mother-of-pearl door panels make it among the world's most decadent libraries. The interior of Phra Mondop is closed to the public.

Phra Mondop, along with the neighbouring Khmer-style peak of the Prasat Phra Thep Bidon and the gilded Phra Si Ratana *chedi* (stupa), are the tallest structures in the compound.

Chakri Mahaprasat

The largest of the palace buildings is the triple-winged Chakri Mahaprasat (Grand Palace Hall). Completed in 1882 following a plan by British architects, the exterior shows a peculiar blend of Italian Renaissance and Thai architecture that earned it the Thai nickname *fa·ràng sài chá·dah* ('Westerner wearing a Thai classical dancer's headdress'). The central spire contains the ashes of Chakri kings; the flanking spires enshrine the ashes of the many Chakri princes who failed to inherit the throne.

Amarindra Hall

Originally a hall of justice, this large, mostly empty hall is used for coronation ceremonies – the most recent occasion being the current king's coronation in 2017. The golden, boat-shaped throne looks considerably more ornate than comfortable.

Borombhiman Hall

This French-inspired structure served as a residence for Rama VI (King Vajiravudh; r 1910–25). The palace was also where Rama VIII (King Ananda Mahidol; r 1935–46) was mysteriously killed in 1946, and in April 1981, General San Chitpatima used it as the headquarters for an attempted coup. Today the structure can only be viewed through iron gates.

Dusit Hall

The compound's westernmost structure is the Ratanakosin-style Dusit Hall, which initially served as a venue for royal audiences and, later, as a royal funerary hall.

Dress for Success

Most of Bangkok's biggest tourist attractions are in fact sacred places and visitors should dress and behave appropriately. In particular, at Wat Phra Kaew and the Grand Palace, you won't be allowed to enter unless you're well covered. Shorts, sleeveless shirts or spaghetti-strap tops, cropped pants – basically anything that reveals more than your arms and head – are not allowed. Those who aren't dressed appropriately can expect to be shown into a dressing room and issued with a sarong before being allowed in.

Wat Phra Kaew and the Grand Palace

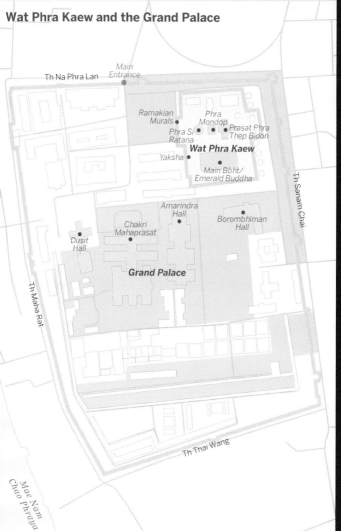

Top Sight 🛕
Wat Pho

Of all Bangkok's temples, Wat Pho is arguably the one most worth visiting, for both its remarkable Reclining Buddha image and its sprawling, stupa-studded grounds. The temple compound boasts a long list of credits: the oldest and largest wát in Bangkok; the longest Reclining Buddha and the largest collection of Buddha images in Thailand; and the country's first public-education institution.

◎ **MAP P44, C5**

วัดโพธิ์/วัดพระเชตุพน, Wat Phra Chetuphon

Th Sanam Chai

admission 100B

🕗 8.30am-6.30pm

🚤 Tien Pier

Reclining Buddha

Located in the compound's main *wí·hǎhn* (sanctuary), the genuinely impressive Reclining Buddha (pictured left), 46m long and 15m high, illustrates the passing of the Buddha into nirvana (ie the Buddha's death). Completed in 1848 and still holding the title of Bangkok's largest Reclining Buddha, the figure is modelled out of plaster around a brick core and is finished in gold leaf. Mother-of-pearl inlay ornaments the feet, displaying the 108 different *lák·sà·nà* (characteristics) of a Buddha. Continuing the numerical theme, behind the statue are 108 bronze monk bowls; for 20B you can buy 108 coins, each of which you then drop in a bowl for good luck.

Phra Ubosot

Though built during the reign of Rama I (King Phraphutthayotfa Chulalok; r 1782–1809) and influenced by the Ayuthaya school of architecture, the *bòht* (ordination hall) as it stands today is the result of extensive renovations dating back to the reign of Rama III (King Phranangklao; r 1824-51). Inside you'll find impressive murals and a three-tiered pedestal supporting Phra Buddha Deva Patimakorn, the compound's second-most noteworthy Buddha statue, as well as the ashes of Rama I.

Other Buddha Statues

The images on display in the four *wí·hǎhn* surrounding Phra Ubosot are worth investigation. Particularly beautiful are the Phra Chinnarat and Phra Chinnasri Buddhas in the western and southern chapels, both rescued from Sukhothai by relatives of Rama I. The galleries extending between the four structures feature no fewer than 394 gilded Buddha images spanning nearly all schools of traditional Thai craftsmanship, from Lopburi to Ko Ratanakosin.

★ Top Tips

○ Arrive early to avoid the crowds and to take advantage of the (relatively) cool weather.

○ Don't just gawk at the Reclining Buddha and call it a day: Wat Pho's fantastical, almost mazelike grounds are also part of the experience, and are home to some less hyped but worthwhile treasures.

✕ Take a Break

○ You'd be wise to combine your visit to Wat Pho with lunch, specifically lunch at Pa Aew (p49), an open-air stall that serves tasty Bangkok-style curries and stir-fries.

○ If you need air-con, consider one of the numerous cafes that line Th Maha Rat.

Ancient Inscriptions

Encircling Phra Ubosot is a low marble wall with 152 bas-reliefs depicting scenes from the *Ramakian*, the Thai version of the *Ramayana*. You'll recognise some of these figures when you exit the temple past the hawkers with mass-produced rubbings for sale: these are made from cement casts based on Wat Pho's reliefs.

Nearby, a small pavilion west of Phra Ubosot has Unesco-awarded inscriptions detailing the tenets of traditional Thai massage. These and as many as 2000 other stone inscriptions covering various aspects of traditional Thai knowledge led to Wat Pho's legacy as Thailand's first public university.

Royal Chedi

On the western side of the grounds is a collection of four towering tiled *chedi* (stupa) commemorating the first four Chakri kings. Note the square bell shape with distinct corners, a signature of Ratanakosin style, and the titles emulating the colours of the Buddhist flag. The middle *chedi* is dedicated to Rama I and encases Phra Si Sanphet Dayarn, a 16m-high standing Buddha image from Ayuthaya. The compound's 91 smaller *chedi* include clusters containing the ashes of lesser royal descendants.

Phra Mondop

Also known as *hŏr đrai*, and serving as a depository for Buddhist scriptures, the elevated Phra Mondop is guarded by four *yaksha* (giants).

Wat Pho

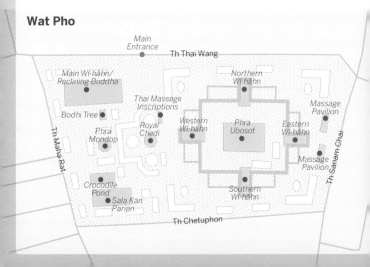

Wat Pho's Granite Statues

Aside from monks and sightseers, Wat Pho is filled with an altogether stiffer crowd: dozens of giants and figurines carved from granite. The rock giants first arrived in Thailand as ballast aboard Chinese junks and were put to work in Wat Pho (and other wát, including Wat Suthat), guarding the entrances of temple gates and courtyards. Look closely and you'll see an array of Chinese characters. The giants with bulging eyes and Chinese opera costumes were inspired by warrior noblemen and are called Lan Than. The figure in a straw hat is a farmer, forever interrupted during his day's work cultivating the fields. And can you recognise the guy in the fedora-like hat with a trimmed beard and moustache? Marco Polo, of course, who introduced such European styles to the Chinese court.

Legend has it that an argument between the four led to the clearing of the area known today as Tha Tien. Just south of the Phra Mondop is the currently reptile-free Crocodile Pond.

Sala Kan Parian

Located in the southwestern corner of the compound is Sala Kan Parian, one of the few remaining structures that predate Rama III's extensive 19th-century renovation/expansion of then Wat Pho Tharam. Built in the Ayuthaya style, the structure formerly functioned as the wát's primary bòht, and held the temple compound's primary Buddha statue.

The Grounds

Small Chinese-style rock gardens and hill islands interrupt the compound's numerous tiled courtyards providing shade, greenery and quirky decorations depicting daily life. Keep an eye out for the distinctive rockery festooned with figures of the hermit Khao Mor – who is credited with inventing yoga – in various healing positions. Directly south of the main wí·hăhn is a Bodhi tree (dôn po), grown from a clipping of the original under which the Buddha is said to have attained enlightenment, and also the source of the temple's colloquial name, Wat Pho.

Top Sight
Wat Arun

The missile-shaped temple that rises from Mae Nam Chao Phraya's banks is known as Temple of Dawn, and was named after the Indian god of dawn, Aruna. It was here that, after the destruction of Ayuthaya, King Taksin stumbled upon a small local shrine and interpreted the discovery as an auspicious sign that this should be the site of the new capital of Siam.

📍 **MAP P44, B6**

วัดอรุณฯ

www.watarun.net

off Th Arun Amarin

admission 50B

🕐 8am-6pm

⛴ cross-river ferry from Tien Pier

The Spire

The central feature of Wat Arun is the 82m-high Khmer-style *prahng* (spire), constructed during the first half of the 19th century by Rama II (King Phraphutthaloetla Naphalai; r 1809–24). From the river it is not apparent that this corn-cob-shaped steeple is adorned with colourful floral murals made of glazed porcelain, a common temple ornamentation in the early Ratanakosin period, when Chinese ships calling at Bangkok used the stuff as ballast. At the time of research, the spire of Wat Arun was closed due to renovation. Visitors can enter the compound, but cannot, as in previous years, climb the tower.

The Ordination Hall

The compound's primary *bòht* (ordination hall) contains a Buddha image that is said to have been designed by Rama II himself, as well as beautiful murals that depict Prince Siddhartha (the Buddha) encountering examples of birth, old age, sickness and death outside his palace walls, experiences that led him to abandon the worldly life.

The Grounds

In addition to the central spire and ordination hall, the Wat Arun compound includes two *wí·hăhn* (sanctuaries) and a *hŏr drai* (depository for Buddhist scriptures), among other structures. Adjacent to the river are six *săhlah* (often spelt as *sala*), open-air pavilions traditionally meant for relaxing or study, but increasingly used these days as docks for tourist boats.

Exploring the Neighbourhood

Many people visit Wat Arun on long-tail boat tours, but it's dead easy and more rewarding to just jump on the 3B cross-river ferry from Tien Pier (from 5am to 9pm). Once across, consider taking a stroll away from the river on Th Wang Doem, a quiet tiled street of wooden shophouses.

★ Top Tips

o You must wear appropriate clothing to visit Wat Arun. If you are flashing too much flesh, you'll have to rent a sarong for 20B (and a 100B refundable deposit).

o To get your money's worth, it's best to visit Wat Arun in the late afternoon, when the sun shines from the west, lighting up the spire and river behind it.

o Sunset views of the temple compound can be caught from across the river at the warehouses that line Th Maha Rat – although be forewarned that locals may ask for a 20B 'fee'.

✕ Take a Break

o Consider a lunch break at Tonkin-Annam (p49), an excellent Vietnamese restaurant just across the river.

o Sunset views of the temple compound can also be seen from Roof or Amorosa (p51), rooftop bars located directly across from the temple.

Walking Tour 🚶

Bangkok's Birthplace

Most of Bangkok's must-see spots are found in the former royal district, Ko Ratanakosin. This walk takes in all of them, plus some lower-key sights. It's wisest to start early to beat the heat and get in before the hordes descend. Dress modestly in order to gain entry to the temples, and politely but firmly ignore any strangers who approach you offering advice on sightseeing or shopping.

Walk Facts

Start Chang Pier

End Wat Arun

Length 4km; three to four hours

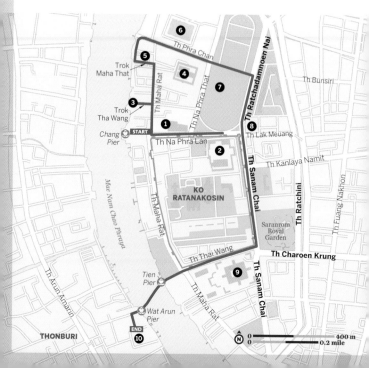

❶ Silpakorn University

Start at Chang Pier and follow Th Na Phra Lan east with a quick diversion to this institution, Thailand's premier **fine-arts university**.

❷ Wat Phra Kaew & Grand Palace

Continue east to the main gate of the famous **Wat Phra Kaew & Grand Palace** (p32).

❸ Trok Tha Wang

Return to Th Maha Rat and proceed north, through a gauntlet of herbal apothecaries and footpath amulet sellers. After passing the cat-laden news stand (you'll know it when you smell it), turn left into **Trok Tha Wang**, a narrow alleyway holding a seemingly hidden classic Bangkok neighbourhood.

❹ Wat Mahathat

Returning to Th Maha Rat, continue moving north. On your right is **Wat Mahathat**, one of Thailand's most respected Buddhist universities.

❺ Amulet Market

Across the street, turn left into crowded Trok Mahathat to see the cramped **Amulet Market** (p51). As you continue north alongside the river, amulet vendors soon give way to food vendors.

❻ Thammasat University

The emergence of white-and-black uniforms is a clue you're approaching **Thammasat University**, which is known for its law and political-science departments.

❼ Sanam Luang

Exiting at Th Phra Chan, cross Th Maha Rat and continue east until you reach **Sanam Luang**, the 'Royal Field'.

❽ Lak Meuang

Cross the field and continue south along Th Ratchadamnoen Nai until you reach the home of the city spirit of Bangkok, **Lak Meuang**.

❾ Wat Pho

Head south along Th Sanam Chai and turn right onto Th Thai Wang, which leads to the entrance of **Wat Pho** (p36), home of the giant reclining Buddha.

❿ Wat Arun

If you've still got the energy, head to adjacent Tha Tien to catch the cross-river ferry to **Wat Arun** (p38), one of the few Buddhist temples you're encouraged to partially climb on.

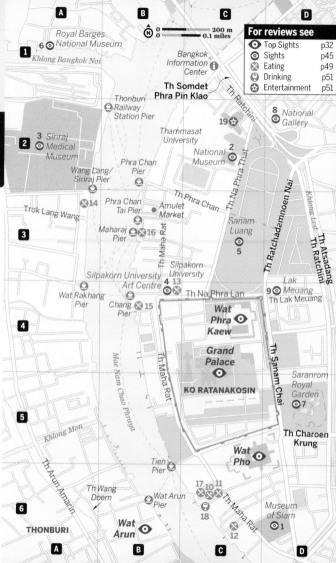

N
0 — 200 m
0 — 0.1 miles

Royal Barges
National Museum
6
1
Khlong Bangkok Noi

Bangkok
Information
Center

Th Somdet
Phra Pin Klao

Thonburi
Railway
Station Pier

3 Siriraj
Medical
Museum
2

Thammasat
University

8 National
Gallery

19

National
Museum
2

Th Ratchini

Th Na Phra That

Wang Lang/
Siriraj Pier

Phra Chan
Pier

Th Phra Chan

Trok Lang Wang

14

Phra Chan
Tai Pier

Amulet
Market

Sanam
Luang
5

Th Ratchadamnoen Nai

Khlong Lo(?)

Th Atsadang
Th Ratchini

Maharaj
Pier
16

Th Maha Rat

Silpakorn
University

Silpakorn University
Art Centre
4 13

Wat Rakhang
Pier

Chang
Pier
15

Th Na Phra Lan

Lak
Meuang
9
Th Lak Meuang

Wat
Phra
Kaew

Grand
Palace

Th Sanam Chai

Saranrom
Royal
Garden
7

KO RATANAKOSIN

Mae Nam Chao Phraya

Khlong Mon

Th Charoen
Krung

Th Arun Amarin

Tien
Pier

Th Wang
Doem

Wat Arun
Pier

Wat
Pho

Wat
Arun

17 10 11
18

12

Th Maha Rat

Museum
of Siam
1

THONBURI

Sights

Museum of Siam
MUSEUM

1  MAP P44, D6

Although temporarily closed for renovation when we stopped by, this fun museum's collection employs explores the origins of the Thai people and their culture. Housed in a European-style 19th-century building, the exhibits are presented in a contemporary and interactive fashion not typically found in Thailand's museums. They are also refreshingly balanced and entertaining, with galleries dealing with a range of questions about the origins of the nation and its people. (สถาบันพิพิธภัณฑ์การเรียนรู้แห่งชาติ; www. museumsiam.org; Th Maha Rat; 300B; ⊙10am-6pm Tue-Sun; 👬, 🚢Tien Pier)

National Museum
MUSEUM

2  MAP P44, C2

Often touted as Southeast Asia's biggest museum, the National Museum is home to an impressive, albeit occasionally dusty, collection of items, best appreciated on one of the museum's free guided **tours** (⊙9.30am Wed & Thu). Most of the museum's structures were built in 1782 as the palace of Rama I's viceroy, Prince Wang Na. Rama V turned it into a museum in 1874 and today there are three permanent exhibitions spread out over several buildings. When we stopped by, several of the exhibition halls were being renovated. (พิพิธภัณฑสถานแห่งชาติ; 4 Th Na Phra That; 200B; ⊙9am-4pm Wed-Sun; 🚢Chang Pier, Maharaj Pier, Phra Chan Tai Pier)

Thai Royal Chariot, National Museum

VASSAMON ANANSUKKASEM/SHUTTERSTOCK ©

Ko Ratanakosin & Thonburi Sights

Siriraj Medical Museum

MUSEUM

3 ⓞ MAP P44, A2

Various appendages, murder weapons and crime-scene evidence, including a bloodied T-shirt from a victim stabbed to death with a dildo, are on display at these linked museums – collectively dubbed the Museum of Death – dedicated to anatomy, pathology and forensic science.The easiest way to reach the Siriraj museum is by taking the river-crossing ferry from Chang Pier to Wang Lang/ Siriraj Pier in Thonburi. At the exit to the pier, turn right (north) to enter Siriraj Hospital and follow the green Museum signs. (พิพิธภัณฑ์ นิติเวชศาสตร์สงกรานต์นิยมเสน; 2nd fl, Adulyadejvikrom Bldg, Siriraj Hospital; 200B; ⏰10am-4pm Wed-Mon; ⛴Wang Lang/Siriraj Pier, Thonburi Railway Station Pier)

Silpakorn University Art Centre

GALLERY

4 ⓞ MAP P44, B4

This gallery – located inside Thailand's most prestigious arts school, **Silpakorn University** (มหาวิทยาลัยศิลปากร; www.su.ac.th; 31 Th Na Phra Lan; ⛴Chang Pier, Maharaj Pier, Phra Chan Tai Pier) – showcases faculty and student exhibitions. There's also an accompanying courtyard cafe and art shop. (หอ ศิลป์มหาวิทยาลัยศิลปากร; www.facebook. com/ArtCentre.SilpakornUniversity; admission free; ⏰9am-7pm Mon-Fri, to 4pm Sat)

Sanam Luang

PARK

5 ⓞ MAP P44, C3

On a hot day, Sanam Luang (Royal Field) is far from charming: a shadeless expanse of dying grass and concrete pavement ringed by flocks of pigeons and homeless people. Yet despite its shabby appearance, it has been at the centre of royal ceremony since Bangkok was founded. (สนามหลวง; bounded by Th Na Phra That, Th Ratchadamnoen Nai & Th Na Phra Lan; ⏰daylight hours; ⛴Chang Pier, Maharaj Pier, Phra Chan Tai Pier)

Royal Barges National Museum

MUSEUM

6 ⓞ MAP P44, A1

The royal barges are slender, fantastically ornamented vessels used in ceremonial processions. The tradition dates back to the Ayuthaya era, when travel (for commoners and royals) was by boat. When not in use, the barges are on display at this Thonburi museum.The most convenient way to get here is by motorcycle taxi from Phra Pin Klao Bridge Pier (ask the driver to go to *reu·a prá têe nâng*). The museum is also an optional stop on long-tail boat trips through Thonburi's canals. (พิพิธภัณฑสถานแห่งชาติเรือพระราชพิธี/ เรือพระที่นั่ง; Khlong Bangkok Noi or 80/1 Th Arun Amarin; admission 100B; camera 100B; ⏰9am-5pm; ⛴Phra Pin Klao Bridge Pier)

Understanding Bangkok's Wáts?

Bangkok is home to hundreds of wáts, temple compounds that have traditionally been at the centre of community life.

Buildings & Structures

Even the smallest wát will usually have a *bòht*, a *wí·hahn* and monks' living quarters.

Bòht The most sacred prayer room at a wát, often similar in size and shape to the *wí·hahn*. Aside from the fact it does not house the main Buddha image, you'll know the *bòht* because it is usually more ornately decorated and has eight cornerstones to mark its boundary.

Chedi (stupa) A large bell-shaped tower usually containing five structural elements symbolising (from bottom to top) earth, water, fire, wind and void; depending on the wát, relics of the Buddha, a Thai king or some other notable are housed inside.

Drum Tower Elevates the ceremonial drum beaten by novices.

Hŏr đrai The manuscript library: a structure for holding Buddhist scriptures. As these texts were previously made from palm leaves, *hŏr đrai* were typically elevated or built over water to protect them from flooding and/or termites.

Mon·dòp An open-sided, square building with four arches and a pyramidal roof, used to worship religious objects or texts.

Prahng A towering phallic spire of Khmer origin serving the same religious purpose as a *chedi*.

Săh·lah (sala) A pavilion, often open-sided, for relaxation, lessons or miscellaneous activities.

Wí·hăhn (vihara) The sanctuary for the temple's main Buddha image and where laypeople come to make their offerings. Classic architecture typically has a three-tiered roof representing the triple gems: the Buddha (the teacher), Dharma (the teaching) and Sangha (the followers).

Saranrom Royal Garden PARK

7 ◉ MAP P44, D5

Easily mistaken for a European public garden, this Victorian-era green space was originally designed as a royal residence in the time of Rama IV. After Rama VII abdicated in 1935, the palace served

Thonburi's Southern Thai Restaurants

The area around Thonburi's Siriraj Hospital is one of the best places in Bangkok for southern Thai food, the theory being that the cuisine took root here because of the nearby train station that served southern destinations. In particular, between Soi 8 and Soi 13 of Th Wang Lang there is a knot of authentic, southern Thai-style curry shops: **Dao Tai** (508/26 Th Wang Lang, no Roman-script sign; mains from 30B; ⏰7am-8.30pm; 🚤Wang Lang/Siriraj Pier), **Ruam Tai** (376/4 Th Wang Lang, no Roman-script sign; mains from 30B; ⏰7am-9pm; 🚤Wang Lang/Siriraj Pier) and **Chawang** (375/5-6 Th Wang Lang; mains from 30B; ⏰7am-7pm; 🚤Wang Lang/Siriraj Pier). A menu isn't necessary as all feature bowls and trays of prepared curries, soups, stir-fries and relishes; simply point to whatever looks tastiest. And when eating, don't feel ashamed if you're feeling the heat; even Bangkok Thais tend to find southern Thai cuisine spicy.

as the headquarters of the People's Party, the political organisation that orchestrated the handover of the government. The open space remained and in 1960 was opened to the public. (สวนสราญรมย์; bounded by Th Ratchini, Th Charoen Krung & Th Sanam Chai; ⏰5am-9pm; 🚤Tien Pier)

National Gallery

GALLERY

8 📍 MAP P44, D2

Housed in a building that was the Royal Mint during the reign of Rama V, the National Gallery's permanent exhibition is admittedly a rather dusty and dated affair. Secular art is a relatively new concept in Thailand and most of the country's best examples of fine art reside in the temples for which they were created – much as historic Western art is often found in European cathedrals. As such, most of the permanent collection here documents Thai-

land's homage to modern styles. (พิพิธภัณฑสถานแห่งชาติหอศิลป์/หอศิลป์ เจ้าฟ้า; www.facebook.com/thenation-algallerythailand; 4 Th Chao Fa; 200B; ⏰9am-4pm Wed-Sun; 🚤Chang Pier, Maharaj Pier, Phra Chan Tai Pier)

Lak Meuang

MONUMENT

9 📍 MAP P44, D4

Serving as the spiritual keystone of Bangkok, Lak Meuang is a phallus-shaped wooden pillar erected by Rama I during the foundation of the city in 1782. Part of an animistic tradition, the city pillar embodies the city's guardian spirit (Phra Sayam Thewathirat) and also lends a practical purpose as a marker of a town's crossroads and measuring point for distances between towns. (ศาลหลักเมือง; cnr Th Sanam Chai & Th Lak Meuang; ⏰6.30am-6.30pm; 🚤Chang Pier, Maharaj Pier, Phra Chan Tai Pier)

Eating

Tonkin-Annam
VIETNAMESE $$

10  MAP P44, C6

The retro-minimalist interior here might be a red flag for hipster ethnic cuisine, but Tonkin-Annam serves some of the best Vietnamese food in Bangkok. Come for the deliciously tart and peppery banana-blossom salad, or dishes you won't find elsewhere. (📞 093 469 2969; www. facebook.com/tonkinannam; 69 Soi Tha Tien; mains 140-300B; ⏰10am-10pm Wed-Mon; ❄; 🚤Tien Pier)

Pa Aew
THAI $

11  MAP P44, C6

Pull up a plastic stool for some rich, seafood-heavy, Bangkok-style fare. It's a bare-bones, open-air curry stall, but for taste, Pa Aew is one of our favourite places to eat in this part of town.There's no English-language sign; look for the exposed trays of food directly in front of the Krung Thai Bank near the corner with Soi Pratu Nokyung. (Th Maha Rat; mains 20-60B; ⏰10am-5pm Tue-Sat; 🚤Tien Pier)

Err
THAI $$

12  MAP P44, C6

Think of all those different smoky, spicy, crispy, meaty bites you've encountered on the street. Now imagine them assembled in one funky, retro-themed locale and coupled with tasty Thai-themed cocktails and domestic micro-brews. (www.errbkk.com; off Th Maha Rat; mains 65-360B; ⏰11am-late Tue-Sun; ❄; 🚤Tien Pier)

Waterfront canal markets (p50)

SORAKRAI TANGNOI/SHUTTERSTOCK ©

Ko Ratanakosin & Thonburi Eating

Ming Lee

THAI, CHINESE $

13 MAP P44, B4

Hidden in plain sight across from Wat Phra Kaew is this decades-old shophouse restaurant. The menu spans Western/Chinese dishes and Thai standards. Often closed before 6pm, Ming Lee is best approached as a post-sightseeing lunch option.There's no English-language sign; look for the last shophouse before Silpakorn University. (28-30 Th Na Phra Lan, mains 70-100B; ⏱11.30am-6pm; 🚤Chang Pier, Maharaj Pier, Phra Chan Tai Pier)

Wang Lang Market

THAI $

14 MAP P44, A3

Running south from Siriraj Hospital is this market bringing together takeaway stalls and basic restaurants. Options range from noodles to curries and, come lunch, the area is positively mobbed by the office staff. (Trok Wang Lang; mains 30-80B; ⏱10am-3pm Mon-Fri; 🚤Wang Lang/Siriraj Pier)

Navy Club

THAI $$

15 MAP P44, B4

The restaurant of the Royal Navy Association has one of the few coveted riverfront locations along this stretch of Mae Nam Chao Phraya. Locals come for the combination of views and tasty seafood-based eats – not for the cafeteria-like atmosphere. (77 Th Maha Rat; mains 70-450B; ⏱11am-10pm; ❄; 🚤Chang Pier, Maharaj Pier, Phra Chan Tai Pier)

Savoey

THAI $$

16 MAP P44, B3

You're not going to find heaps of character at this chain restaurant (with other branches across town), but you will get consistency, river views, air-con and a seafood-heavy menu that should appeal. Come cool evenings, take advantage of the open-air, riverside deck. (www.savoey.co.th; 1st fl, Maharaj Pier, Th Maha Rat; mains 125-1800B; ⏱10am-10pm; ❄; 🚤Maharaj Pier, Chang Pier)

Exploring Thonburi's Canals

For an up-close view of Thonburi's canals, long-tail boats are available for charter at Tha Chang and Tha Tien from 8.30am to 5pm. Trips explore **Khlong Bangkok Noi** and **Khlong Bangkok Yai**, taking in the Royal Barges National Museum, Wat Arun and a riverside temple with fish feeding. Longer excursions make side trips into **Khlong Mon**, between Bangkok Noi and Bangkok Yai and, on weekends, include a stop at the floating market at Taling Chan. However, it's worth pointing out that the most common tour of one hour (1000B, up to eight people) does not allow enough time to disembark and explore any of these sights. To do so, you'll need 1½ hours (1300B) or two hours (1500B).

Sala Rattanakosin Eatery & Bar

THAI $$$

17 🍽 MAP P44, C6

Located on an open-air deck next to the river with Wat Arun virtually towering overhead, the Sala Rattanakosin hotel's signature restaurant has nailed the location. The food – largely central and northern Thai dishes with occasional Western twists – doesn't necessarily live up to the scenery. (📞02 622 1388; www.salaresorts.com/rattanako sin; Sala Rattanakosin, 39 Th Maha Rat; mains 240-1100B; ⏰11am-4.30pm & 5.30-11pm; ❄; 🚢Tien Pier)

Drinking

Roof

BAR

The open-air bar on top of the Sala Rattanakosin hotel (see 17 🍽 Map p44, C6) has upped the stakes for sunset views of Wat Arun – if you can see the temple at all through the wall of selfie-snapping tourists. Be sure to get there early for a good seat. (5th fl, Sala Rattanakosin; ⏰5pm-midnight Mon-Thu, to 1am Fri-Sun)

Amorosa

BAR

18 🍺 MAP P44, C6

Perched above the Arun Residence, Amorosa takes advantage of a location directly above the river and opposite Wat Arun. The cocktails aren't going to blow you away, but watching boats ply their way along the royal river as Wat Arun glows is a beautiful reminder that you're not home any more. (www.arunresidence. com; rooftop, Arun Residence, 36-38 Soi

Amulet Market

Bangkok's arcane **market** (ตลาด พระเครื่องวัดมหาธาตุ; Map p44, B3; Th Maha Rat; ⏰7am-5pm; 🚢Chang Pier, Maharaj Pier, Phra Chan Tai Pier) claims both the footpaths along Th Maha Rat and Th Phra Chan, as well as a network of covered market stalls that runs south from Phra Chan Pier (the easiest entry point is clearly marked 'Trok Maha That'). The trade is based around small talismans carefully prized by collectors, monks, taxi drivers and people in dangerous professions.

Pratu Nokyung; ⏰5pm-midnight Mon-Thu, to 1am Fri-Sun; 🚢Tien Pier)

Entertainment

National Theatre

THEATRE

19 ⭐ MAP P44, C2

The National Theatre holds performances of *kŏhn* (masked dance-drama based on stories from the *Ramakian*) at 2pm on the first and second Sundays of the month from January to September, and *lá-kon* (classical dance-dramas) at 2pm on the first and second Sundays of the month from October to December. Tickets go on sale an hour before performances begin. (📞02 224 1342; 2 Th Ratchini; tickets 60-100B; 🚢Chang Pier, Maharaj Pier, Phra Chan Tai Pier)

Explore
Banglamphu

Antique shophouses, ancient temples: Banglamphu is old Bangkok encapsulated in one leafy, breezy district. It's worth sticking around Banglamphu for lunch, as this is when the majority of the area's street stalls and shophouse restaurants are operating. Come evening, young locals flood the area in search of cheap eats, giving it an entirely different vibe.

Start your day with a bird's-eye view of the area from the Golden Mount (p58). Descend and learn about the unique local trade at nearby Ban Baat (p60). Continue by foot to the impressive but little-visited Wat Suthat (p58). For lunch, try classic Bangkok-style restaurants such as Krua Apsorn (p62). After refuelling, cross over to Th Khao San, taking in the famous district's hectic street market (p72). Come evening, consider watching a Thai boxing match at Rajadamnern Stadium (p70) or partying with local hipsters at Hippie de Bar (p70) or Phra Nakorn Bar & Gallery (p70).

Getting There & Around

Banglamphu is not very well linked up with the rest of the city by public transport networks. During the day, a good strategy is to approach the area via the river ferry at Phra Athit/Banglamphu Pier. At night, most of the action is centred on Th Khao San, which can be accessed via taxi from the BTS stop at National Stadium or the MRT stop at Hua Lamphong.

- 🚤 **Chao Phraya Express Boat** Phra Athit/Banglamphu Pier.
- 🚤 **Klorng boat** Phanfa Leelard Pier.

Neighbourhood Map on p56

Túk-túk, Banglamphu AMNAT30/SHUTTERSTOCK ©

Walking Tour 🥾

Banglamphu Pub Crawl

You don't need to go far to find a decent bar in Banglamphu – it's one of Bangkok's best nightlife hoods – but why limit yourself to one? With this in mind, we've assembled a pub crawl that spans river views, people-watching, live music and late-night shenanigans.

Walk Facts

Start Sheepshank; 🚤 Tha Phra Athit/Banglamphu

End The Bank; 🚤 Tha Phra Athit/Banglamphu

Length 2km; three to six hours

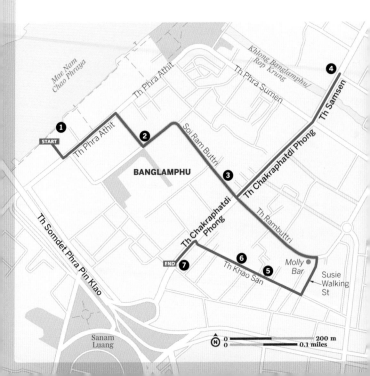

❶ River Views

Begin your crawl in sophisti-cated, air-conditioned comfort at **Sheepshank** (📞02 629 5165; www. sheepshankpublichouse.com; 47 Th Phra Athit; mains 320-1150B; ⏰6pm-midnight Tue-Sat; ❄), a gastropub with an intriguing menu of bar snacks and classic cocktails, or *en plein air* at **Babble & Rum** (www. nexthotels.com/hotel/riva-surya -bangkok; Riva Surya hotel, 23 Th Phra Athit; ⏰5-10).

❷ People-watching

Cross over to Soi Ram Buttri for **Gecko Bar** (cnr Soi Chana Songkh-ram & Soi Ram Buttri; ⏰10am-1am), a cheap, low-key spot from which to gawk at passers-by, or a few doors down, **Madame Musur** (p68) offers the same perks, but with a bit more sophistication and northern-style Thai dishes.

❸ Urban Beach

There seems to be a current (and inexplicable) trend for beach-themed, almost tiki-bar-style pubs in Banglamphu. If this aesthetic appeals, head south on Soi Ram Buttri and hunker down with a fruity cocktail among the Easter Island heads and bamboo decor at **Sawasdee House** (147 Soi Ram Buttri; ⏰11am-2am) or, just south of Th Chakraphadti Phong, **Macaroni Club** (36 Th Rambuttri; ⏰24hr).

❹ Live Music

Every pub crawl requires at least one singalong to a cheesy covers soundtrack (if you haven't yet heard a live version of 'Hotel California', you haven't really been to Bangkok), so head north on Th Chakraphadti Phong to the longstanding blues bar **Ad Here the 13th** (p71) or to one of the open-air live-music bars along Th Rambuttri, such as **Molly Bar** (108 Th Rambuttri; ⏰8pm-1am;).

❺ Th Khao San

At this point, you should be sufficiently lubricated for the main event: Th Khao San. Get a bird's-eye view of the multina-tional backpacker parade from the elevated **Roof Bar** (Th Khao San; ⏰5pm-midnight) or from street level at the noisy and buzzy **Center Khao Sarn** (Th Khao San; ⏰24hr), roughly across the street.

❻ Dance Fever

If you can muster the energy, it's probably the right time to hit one of Th Khao San's nightclubs such as the **The Club** (p68). Don't bother checking in before midnight.

❼ Late Night

If 2am (the closing time of most bars in the area) is too early, crawl over to **The Bank** (3rd fl, 44 Th Chakraphadti Phong; ⏰6pm-late), a rooftop lounge and nightclub that stays open late – very late. Don't say we didn't warn you…

A

B

C

D

Soi 3

1

Phra Sumen Fort & 7
Santi Chai Prakan Park ◎

17 ✗

Khong Banglamphu Khlong Rop Krung

Soi 1

Soi 6

Th Samsen

Soi 4

21 ✗

Phra Athit/
Banglamphu Pier ✗26

✗25

45

20

Pua-
Kee

Th Phra Athit

37 ✗

18 ✗

Mae Nam
Chao Phraya

31 ✗
✗29
24
39

BANGLAMPHU

Th Phra Sumen

Th Phra Athit

27
23

Soi Ram Buttri

Th Chakraphatdi Phong

Th Kraisi

◎5

Th Sipahm
Hang

Wat
Bowonniwe

2

Soi Chana
Songkhram

44

Th Tani

Th Somdet Phra Pin Klao

Th Rongmai

Th Ratchini

Wat Chana
Songkhram

Th Kasab

✗15

Th Rambuttri

3

National
Theatre

National
Museum

30
33

Trok
Mayom

Th Khao San

40
34

Susie
Walking St

43

May
Kaidee's

Soi Damnoen Klang Neua

Th Tanao

Th Ratchadamnoen Klang

4

Thammasat
University

Th Na Phra That

Th Ratchadamnoen Nai

Th Atsadang

Th Ratchini

Soi Damnoen
Klang Tai

32

◎10

October 14
Memorial

Trok Sake

5

Wat
Mahathat

Th Na Phra That

Sanam
Luang

Khlong Lxt

Th Buranasat

Th Mahanop

Soi Nava

Th Tanao

Th Na Phra Lan

Th Lak Meuang

Th Phraeng
Phuthon

6

KO RATANAKOSIN

Th Sanam Chai

Th Kanlaya Namit

41
19
22

42

Th Bamrung Meuang

A

B

C

D

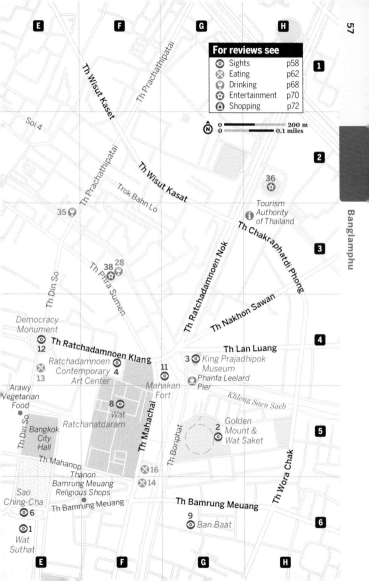

Banglamphu

E **F** **G** **H**

1

Th Wisut Kaset

Th Prachathipatai

For reviews see

◉ Sights	p58
✕ Eating	p62
🍷 Drinking	p68
★ Entertainment	p70
🛍 Shopping	p72

Soi 4

2

36 ★

Th Wisut Kasat

Trok Bahn Lo

ⓝ 0 ————— 200 m
0 ————— 0.1 miles

Tourism
ⓘ Authority
of Thailand

Th Chakraphatdi Phong

35 🍷

Th Prachathipatai

3

Th Ratchadamnoen Nok

Th Nakhon Sawan

38 ★ 28 ◉

Th Phra Sumen

Th Din So

Democracy
Monument

12 ◉

4

Th Ratchadamnoen Klang

Th Lan Luang

3 ◉ King Prajadhipok
Museum

Ratchadamnoen
Contemporary
Art Center

13 ✕

4 ◉

11 ◉

Mahakan
Fort

◉ Phanfa Leelard
Pier

Khlong Saen Saeb

Arawy
Vegetarian
Food

8 ◉

Wat
Ratchanatdaram

Golden
Mount &
Wat Saket

5

Th Din So

Bangkok
City
Hall

Th Mahanop

Th Mahachai

2 ◉

Th Boriphat

Thanon
Bamrung Meuang
Religious Shops

✕16

✕14

Sao
Ching-Cha

6 ◉

Th Bamrung Meuang

Th Bamrung Meuang

Th Wora Chak

6

9 ◉ Ban Baat

1 ◉

Wat
Suthat

E **F** **G** **H**

Sights

Wat Suthat BUDDHIST TEMPLE

1 MAP P56, E6

Other than being just plain huge and impressive, Wat Suthat also holds the highest royal temple grade. Inside the *wí·hǎhn* (sanctuary for a Buddha sculpture) are intricate *Jataka* (stories of the Buddha) murals and the 8m-high **Phra Si Sakayamuni**, Thailand's largest surviving Sukhothai-period bronze, cast in the former capital of Sukhothai in the 14th century. Today the ashes of Rama VIII (King Ananda Mahidol; r 1935–46) are contained in the base of the image. (วัดสุทัศน์; Th Bamrung Meuang; 20B; ☺8.30am-9pm; ⛴klorng boat to Phanfa Leelard Pier)

Golden Mount & Wat Saket BUDDHIST TEMPLE

2 MAP P56, G5

Even if you're wát-ed out, you should tackle the brisk ascent to the Golden Mount (Phu Khao Thong). Serpentine steps wind through an artificial hill shaded by gnarled trees and past graves and

Taking the Boat

Traffic in Bangkok's old town can be brutal, and boats – both the Chao Phraya Express Boat and the *klorng* boats – are a steady, if slow, way to reach Banglamphu.

pictures of wealthy benefactors. At the peak, you'll find a breezy 360°-degree view of Bangkok's most photogenic side.Next door, seemingly peaceful Wat Saket contains murals that are among both the most beautiful and the goriest in the country; proceed to the pillar behind the Buddha statue for explicit depictions of Buddhist hell. (ภูเขาทอง & วัดสระเกศ; admission to summit of Golden Mount 10B; ☺7.30am-5.30pm; ⛴klorng boat to Phanfa Leelard Pier)

King Prajadhipok Museum MUSEUM

3 MAP P56, G4

This museum assembles old photos and memorabilia to illustrate the rather dramatic life of Rama VII (King Prajadhipok; r 1925–35), Thailand's last absolute monarch. It occupies a grand neocolonial-style building constructed on the orders of Rama V for his favourite firm of Bond St merchants – the only foreign business allowed on the royal road linking Bangkok's two palace districts. (พิพิธภัณฑ์พระบาทสมเด็จพระปกเกล้าเจ้าอยู่หัว; www.kingprajadhipok-museum.org; 2 Th Lan Luang; admission free; ☺9am-4pm Tue-Sun; ⛴klorng boat to Phanfa Leelard Pier)

Ratchadamnoen Contemporary Art Center GALLERY

4 MAP P56, F4

This new, three-storey structure hosts changing exhibitions of

Murals, Wat Bowonniwet

mixed-media contemporary domestic art. (หอศิลป์ร่วมสมัย ราชดำเนิน, RCAC; www.facebook.com/Ratchadamnone; Th Ratchadamnoen Klang; admission free; ⏰10am-7pm Tue-Sun; 🚤klorng boat to Phanfa Leelard Pier)

Wat Bowonniwet BUDDHIST TEMPLE

5 ◉ MAP P56, D3

Founded in 1826, Wat Bowonniwet (known colloquially as Wat Bowon) is the national headquarters for the Thammayut monastic sect, a reformed version of Thai Buddhism. The rest of us should visit the temple for the noteworthy murals in its *bòht* (ordination hall), which include Thai depictions of Western life (possibly copied from magazine illustrations) during the early 19th century. Because of its royal status, visitors should be particularly careful to dress properly for admittance; shorts and sleeveless clothing are not allowed. (วัดบวรนิเวศวิหาร; www.watbowon.org; Th Phra Sumen; admission free; ⏰8.30am-5pm; 🚤Phra Athit/Banglamphu Pier)

Sao Ching-Cha MONUMENT

6 ◉ MAP P56, E6

This spindly red arch – a symbol of Bangkok – formerly hosted a Brahman festival in honour of Shiva, in which participants would swing in ever-higher arcs in an effort to reach a bag of gold suspended from a 15m-high bamboo pole. Whoever grabbed the gold could keep it, but that was no mean

feat and deaths were as common
as successes. A black-and-white
photo illustrating the risky rite can
be seen at the ticket counter at
adjacent Wat Suthat. (เสาชิงช้า, Giant
Swing; Th Bamrung Meuang; 🚤klorng
boat to Phanfa Leelard Pier)

Phra Sumen Fort & Santi Chai Prakan Park NOTABLE BUILDING, PARK

7 ◎ MAP P56, B1

Formerly the site of a sugar factory, today Santi Chai Prakan Park
is a tiny patch of greenery with a
great river view and lots of evening
action, including comical commu-
nal aerobics classes. The riverside
pathway heading southwards
makes for a serene promenade.
The park's most prominent
landmark is the blindingly white
Phra Sumen Fort, which was built
in 1783 to defend the city against
a river invasion. (ป้อมพระสุเมรุ, สวน
สันติชัยปราการ; Th Phra Athit; admission free; ⏱5am-9pm; 🚤Phra Athit/
Banglamphu Pier)

Wat Ratchanatdaram BUDDHIST TEMPLE

8 ◎ MAP P56, F5

This temple was built for Rama III
(King Phranangklao; r 1824-51)
in the 1840s. Its design is said to
derive from metal temples built
in India and Sri Lanka more than
2000 years ago. (วัดราชนัดดาราม; Th
Mahachai; admission free; ⏱8am-
5pm; 🚤klorng boat to Phanfa Leelard
Pier)

Ban Baat AREA

9 ◎ MAP P56, G6

The residents of Ban Baat inhabit
the only remaining village of three
established in Bangkok by Rama I
(King Phraphutthayotfa Chulalok;
r 1782–1809) to produce bàht,
the distinctive bowls used by
monks to receive morning food
donations. Tourists – not temples
– are among the customers these
days, and a bowl purchase is
usually rewarded with a bowl-
making demonstration. (บ้านบาตร,
Monk's Bowl Village; off Soi Ban Bat;
⏱9am-5pm; 🚤klorng boat to Phanfa
Leelard Pier)

October 14 Memorial MONUMENT

10 ◎ MAP P56, D4

A peaceful amphitheatre com-
memorates the civilian demonstrators who were killed by the
military during a prodemocracy
rally on 14 October 1973. Over
200,000 people had assembled
at the Democracy Monument and
along the length of Th Ratchadamnoen to protest against the
arrest of political campaigners and
continuing military dictatorship.
Although some in Thailand continue to deny it, photographs confirm
that more than 70 demonstrators
were killed when the tanks met
the crowd. (อนุสรณ์สถาน ๑๔ ตุลา; cnr
Th Ratchadamnoen Klang & Th Tanao;
admission free; ⏱24hr; 🚤klorng boat
to Phanfa Leelard Pier)

Taking a Walk Down Thanon Khao San

Th Khao San, better known as Khao San Rd, is unlike anywhere else on earth. It's a clearing house of people either entering the liberated state of travelling in Southeast Asia or returning to the coddling bonds of first-world life, all coming together in a neon-lit melting pot in Banglamphu. Its uniqueness is best illustrated by this question: apart from airports, where else could you share space with the citizens of dozens of countries, ranging from first-time backpackers scoffing banana pancakes to 75-year-old grandparents ordering G&Ts, and everyone in between?

The Emergence of an Icon

Th Khao San (cow-sarn), meaning 'uncooked rice', is perhaps the highest-profile bastard child of the age of independent travel. Of course, it hasn't always been this way. For its first two centuries it was just an unremarkable road in old Bangkok. The first guesthouses appeared in 1982 and as more backpackers arrived through the '80s, the old wooden homes were converted one by one into low-rent dosshouses. By the time Alex Garland's novel *The Beach* was published in 1997, with its opening scenes set on the seedier side of Khao San, staying here had become a rite of passage for backpackers coming to Southeast Asia.

The Khao San of Today

Publicity from Garland's book and the movie that followed pushed Khao San into the mainstream, romanticising the seediness and stereotyping the backpackers it attracted as unwashed and counterculturalist. It also brought the long-simmering debate about the relative merits of Th Khao San to the top of backpacker conversations. Was it cool to stay on KSR? Was it uncool? Was this 'real travel' or just an international anywhere surviving on the few baht Western backpackers spent before they headed home to start high-earning careers? Was it really Thailand at all? Perceptions aside, today the strip continues to anticipate every traveller's need: meals to soothe homesickness, cafes and bars for swapping travel tales, tailors, travel agents, teeth whitening, secondhand books, hair braiding and, of course, the perennial Akha women trying to harass everyone they see into buying those croaking wooden frogs.

Vegging Out in Banglamphu

Due to the strong foreign influence, there's an abundance of vegetarian restaurants in the Banglamphu area. In addition to Hemlock and Shoshana, both of which have generous meat-free sections, vegetarian alternatives include the following:

Arawy Vegetarian Food (Map p57, E5; 152 Th Din So; mains from 30B; ⏱7am-8pm; 🥢; 🚣 klorng boat to Phanfa Leelard Pier)

Thamna (175 Th Samsen; mains 100-290B; ⏱11am-3pm & 5-9pm Mon-Sat; ❄ 🥢; 🚣Thewet Pier)

May Kaidee's (Map p56, D3; www.maykaidee.com; 59 Th Tanao; mains 80-120B; ⏱9am-10pm; ❄ 🥢; 🚣Phra Athit/Banglamphu Pier)

Mahakan Fort
NOTABLE BUILDING

11 ◉ MAP P56, G4

Dating back to the late 18th century, whitewashed Mahakan Fort is one of two surviving citadels that defended the old walled city. The octagonal fort is a picturesque, if brief and hot, stop en route to Golden Mount, but the neighbouring village is more interesting. This small community of wooden houses has been here for more than 100 years, but since the mid-1990s it has fought the Bangkok municipal government's plan to demolish it and create a 'tourist' park. (ป้อมมหากาฬ; Th Ratchadamnoen Klang; admission free; ⏱24hr; 🚣klorng boat to Phanfa Leelard Pier)

Democracy Monument
MONUMENT

12 ◉ MAP P56, E4

The Democracy Monument is the focal point of the grand, European-style boulevard that is Th Ratchadamnoen Klang. As the name suggests, it was erected to commemorate Thailand's momentous transformation from absolute to constitutional monarchy. (อนุสาวรีย์ประชาธิปไตย; Th Ratchadamnoen Klang; 🚣klorng boat to Phanfa Leelard Pier)

Eating

Krua Apsorn
THAI $$

13 ✕ MAP P56, E4

This cafeteria-like dining room is a favourite of members of the Thai royal family and restaurant critics alike. Just about all of the central and southern Thai dishes are tasty, but regulars never miss the chance to order the decadent stir-fried crab with yellow pepper chili or the *tortilla española*–like fluffy crab omelette. (www.kruaapsorn.com; Th Din So; mains 100-450B; ⏱10.30am-8pm Mon-Sat; ❄; 🚣klorng boat to Phanfa Leelard Pier)

Jay Fai   THAI $$$

14  MAP P56, F6

With its bare-bones dining room, it's
hard to believe Jay Fai is renowned
for serving Bangkok's most expensive *pàt kêe mow* ('drunkard's noodles': wide rice noodles fried with
seafood and Thai herbs). The price,
however, is justified by the copious
fresh seafood, plus a distinct frying
style resulting in an almost oil-free
finished dish. It's in a virtually
unmarked shophouse, opposite a
7-Eleven. (327 Th Mahachai; mains 180-
1000B; ⏰3pm-2am Mon-Sat; 🛥klorng
boat to Phanfa Leelard Pier)

Shoshana   ISRAELI $$

15  MAP P56, C3

One of Khao San's longest-
running Israeli restaurants,
Shoshana resembles your grandparents' living room right down
to the tacky wall art and plastic
placemats. Feel safe in ordering
anything deep-fried – staff do
an excellent job of it – and don't
miss the deliciously garlicky
eggplant dip. (88 Th Chakraphatdi
Phong; mains 80-320B; ⏰10am-
midnight; ❄🖥; 🛥Phra Athit/
Banglamphu Pier)

Thip Samai   THAI $

16  MAP P56, F5

Brace yourself: you should be
aware that the fried noodles sold
from carts along Th Khao San have
little to do with the dish known as
pàt tai. Luckily, less than a five-
minute túk-túk ride away lies Thip
Samai, home to some of the most
legendary fried noodles in town.

Democracy Monument

Banglamphu Eating

Note that Thip Samai is closed on alternate Wednesdays. (313 Th Mahachai; mains 50-250B; ⏱5pm-2am; 🚤klorng boat to Phanfa Leelard Pier)

Somsong Phochana THAI $

17 ❌ MAP P56, C1

This is one of the few places in Bangkok that serves *gŏo·ay dĕe·o sù·kŏh·tai*, or Sukhothai-style noodles: barbecued pork and thin rice noodles in a clear broth seasoned with a little sugar, supplemented with sliced green beans, and garnished with ground peanuts.There's no English-language sign. To find Somsong, enter Th Lamphu, then take the first left, opposite Watsungwej School; the restaurant is on the right. (off Th Lamphu; mains from 30B; ⏱9.30am-4pm; 🚤Phra Athit/Banglamphu Pier)

Baan Nual THAI $$

18 ❌ MAP P56, D1

It's come full circle: the restaurateurs of today are designing venues that resemble the holes-in-the-wall of yesteryear. With three tables and retro charm in spades, Baan Nual is the epitome of this trend. But rest assured that the rich, rather meaty central Thai fare delivers. The English-language menu is limited, but you can hop onto the restaurant's Instagram feed (@baannual372) for more options. (📞081 889 7403; 372 Soi 2, Th Samsen, no Roman-script sign; mains 70-390B; ⏱noon-9pm Tue-Fri, 4-9pm Sat & Sun; 🚤Phra Athit/Banglamphu Pier)

Street food on Th Ratchadamnoen

A Noodle Tour of Thanon Phra Athit

Despite being virtually next door to touristy Th Khao San, Th Phra Athit remains a microcosm of noodle dishes from Bangkok – and beyond. If you're interested in sampling some of Thailand's more obscure noodle dishes, consider one of the following:

Soy (p66) One of the best options for big, hearty bowls of beef noodle soup. Sample the fall-apart tender braised beef, fresh beef, beef balls, or all of the above.

Khun Daeng (p68) This place is renowned for its *gŏo·ay jáp yoo·an*, which you'll find on the English-language menu as 'Vietnamese noodle'. Introduced to northeastern Thailand via Vietnamese immigrants, the dish is a tasty combination of delicious pork sausage, a quail egg, thin rice noodles and a garnish of crispy fried shallots in a slightly viscous broth.

Somsong Phochana Here you'll find *gŏo·ay dĕe·o sù·kŏh·tai*, Sukhothai-style noodles: slices of barbecued pork with thin rice noodles in a clear pork broth seasoned with a little sugar, and served with green beans and ground peanuts. Delish!

Pua-Kee (Map p56, C1; Th Phra Sumen, no Roman-script sign; mains 50-90B; ⏰ 9am-4pm; 🚤 Phra Athit/Banglamphu Pier) Give Pua Kee a visit for the central Thai classic, *gŏo·ay dĕe·o dôm yam* ('rice noodle soup hotspicy with mixed ball' on the menu), fish-ball noodles preaseasoned with sugar, lime and dried chilli, and served with a crispy deep-fried wonton. There's no English-language sign here, but it's located next door to the clearly labelled Makalin Clinic.

Nuttaporn

THAI $

19 ⊗ MAP P56, C6

A crumbling shophouse that for the last 70 years has been churning out some of Bangkok's most famous coconut ice cream – in our opinion, the ideal palate cleanser after a bowl of spicy noodles. Other uniquely domestic flavours include mango, Thai tea and, for the daring, durian. (94 Th Phraeng Phuthon;

mains from 20B; ⏰ 9am-4pm Mon-Sat; 🚶; 🚤 Phra Athit/Banglamphu Pier)

Karim Roti-Mataba

THAI $

20 ⊗ MAP P56, C1

This classic Bangkok eatery may have grown a bit too big for its britches in recent years, but it still serves tasty Thai-Muslim dishes such as roti, *gaang mát·sà·màn* ('Muslim curry'), tart fish curry and *má·dà·bà* (something of a stuffed pancake). An upstairs air-con dining area and a couple of outdoor tables provide barely enough seating for loyal fans and curious tourists alike. (136 Th Phra Athit; mains 40-130B; ⏰9am-10pm Tue-Sun; ❄🍴; 🚤Phra Athit/Banglamphu Pier)

Bangkok Poutine
INTERNATIONAL $$

21 🍴 MAP P56, D1

You've conquered the deep-fried scorpion, now wrangle with poutine: French fries topped with cheese curds and gravy. Run by guys from Québec, this is the place to go for Francophone pop and the latest hockey game, as well as dishes ranging in cuisine from Thai to Lebanese, including lots of meat-free items. (www.facebook.com/bangkokpoutine; Th Samsen; mains 70-200B; ⏰noon-midnight Tue-Sun; ❄🍴; 🚤Phra Athit/Banglamphu Pier)

Off the Beaten Track

Although Th Khao San remains associated with foreign tourists, in recent years it's also become a popular nightlife destination for young locals. For an almost entirely local drinking scene, check out the live-music pubs along Th Phra Athit.

Chote Chitr
THAI $

22 🍴 MAP P56, C6

This third-generation shophouse restaurant boasting just six tables is a Bangkok foodie landmark. The kitchen can be inconsistent and the service is consistently grumpy, but when they're on, dishes like *mèe gròrp* (crispy fried noodles) and *yam tòo·a ploo* (wing-bean salad) are in a class of their own. (146 Th Phraeng Phuthon; mains 60-200B; ⏰11am-10pm; 🚤klorng boat to Phanfa Leelard Pier)

Hemlock
THAI $$

23 🍴 MAP P56, B2

Taking full advantage of its cosy shophouse location, this perennial favourite has enough style to feel like a special night out, but doesn't skimp on flavour or preparation. The eclectic menu reads like an ancient literary work, reviving old dishes from aristocratic kitchens across the country, not to mention several meat-free items. (56 Th Phra Athit; mains 75-280B; ⏰4pm-midnight Mon-Sat; ❄🍴; 🚤Phra Athit/Banglamphu Pier)

Soy
CHINESE $

24 🍴 MAP P56, B2

Long-standing and lauded Soy serves big, hearty bowls of beef noodle soup. Choose between the fall-apart tender braised beef, fresh beef, beef balls, or all of the above.There's no English-language sign here; look for the

Pàt tai: classic Thai rice noodle dish

open-fronted shophouse with red plastic chairs. (100/2-3 Th Phra Athit, no Roman-script sign; mains 80-100B; ⏰7am-5.30pm; 🚤Phra Athit/Banglamphu Pier)

Escapade Burgers & Shakes
AMERICAN $$

25 ⊗ MAP P56, B2

Escapade is proof that, where it concerns US food, Thais have moved light years beyond McDonald's. Squeeze into the narrow, bar-like dining room for messy burgers with edgy ingredients such as 'toasted rice mayo', not to mention some pretty decadent milkshakes. (112 Th Phra Athit; mains 120-330B; ⏰4pm-midnight Tue-Sun; ❄; 🚤Phra Athit/Banglamphu Pier)

Rarb
THAI $$$

26 ⊗ MAP P56, B1

Sip a potent R-rated cocktail (whose name might make you blush) crafted by award-winning bartender Karn Liangsrisuk, formerly of the next-door burger institution Escapade, while '70s Thai funk plays. This resto-bar is tiny, but its *làhp mŏo* (spicy pork salad) is outstanding when paired with house-toasted rice and the chef's secret blend of spices and chillies. A truly local joint in an up-and-coming hood. (49 Th Phra Athit; mains 300-500B; ⏰5pm-midnight Tue-Sun; Ⓢ Saphan Taksin)

Khun Daeng
THAI $

27 🍽 MAP P56, B2

This popular place does *gŏo·ay jáp yoo·an*, identified on the English-language menu as 'Vietnamese noodle'. Introduced to northeastern Thailand via Vietnamese immigrants, the dish combines peppery pork sausage, a quail egg, thin rice noodles and a garnish of crispy fried shallots in a slightly viscous broth. There's no English-language sign here; look for the white-and-green shopfront. (Th Phra Athit, no Roman-script sign; mains 45-55B; ⏰11am-9.30pm Mon-Sat; 🚢Phra Athit/Banglamphu Pier)

Drinking

Ku Bar
BAR

28 🍸 MAP P56, F3

Tired of buckets and cocktails that revolve around Red Bull? Head to Ku Bar, in almost every way the polar opposite of the Khao San party scene. Climb three floors of stairs (look for the tiny sign) to emerge at an almost comically minimalist interior where sophisticated fruit- and food-heavy cocktails (sample names: Lychee, Tomato, Pineapple/ Red Pepper) and obscure music augment the underground vibe. (www.facebook.com/ku.bangkok; 3rd fl, 469 Th Phra Sumen; ⏰7pm-midnight Thu-Sun)

Madame Musur
BAR

29 🍸 MAP P56, B2

Saving you the trip north to Pai, Madame Musur pulls off that elusive combination of northern Thailand meets *The Beach* meets Th Khao San. It's a fun place to chat, drink and people-watch, and it's also not a bad place to eat, with a short menu of northern Thai dishes priced from 100B to 200B. (www.facebook.com/madamemusur; 41 Soi Ram Buttri; ⏰8am-midnight; 🚢Phra Athit/Banglamphu Pier)

The Club
CLUB

30 🍸 MAP P56, C3

Located right in the middle of Th Khao San, this cavern-like dance hall hosts a good mix of locals and backpackers; check the Facebook page for upcoming events and guest DJs. (www.facebook.com/ theclubkhaosanbkk; 123 Th Khao San; admission Fri & Sat 120B; ⏰9pm-2am; 🚢Phra Athit/Banglamphu Pier)

Commé
BAR

31 🍸 MAP P56, B2

The knot of vintage motorcycles is your visual cue, but most likely you'll hear Commé before you see it. A staple for local hipsters, this classic Th Phra Athit semi-open-air bar is the place to go for a loud, boozy, Thai-style night out. (100/4-5 Th Phra Athit; ⏰6pm-1am; 🚢Phra Athit/Banglamphu Pier)

Understand:
Thai Boxing

More formally known as Phahuyut (from the Pali-Sanskrit *bhahu*, meaning 'arm', and *yodha*, 'combat'), Thailand's ancient martial art of *moo·ay tai* (Thai boxing; also spelt *muay Thai*) is one of the kingdom's most striking national icons.

An Ancient Tradition

Many martial-arts aficionados agree that *moo·ay tai* is the most efficient, effective and generally unbeatable form of ring-centred, hand-to-hand combat practised today. After the Siamese were defeated at Ayuthaya in 1767, several expert *moo·ay boh·rahn* (from which contemporary *moo·ay tai* is derived) fighters were among the prisoners hauled off to Burma. A few years later a festival was held; one of the Thai fighters, Nai Khanom Tom, was ordered to take on prominent Burmese boxers for the entertainment of the king and to determine which martial art was most effective. He promptly dispatched nine opponents in a row and, as legend has it, was offered money or beautiful women as a reward; he promptly took two new wives.

The Modern Game

In the early days of the sport, combatants' fists were wrapped in thick horsehide for maximum impact with minimum knuckle damage; tree bark and seashells were used to protect the groin from lethal kicks. But the high incidence of death and physical injury led the Thai government to ban *moo·ay tai* in the 1920s; in the 1930s the sport was revived under a modern set of regulations. Bouts were limited to five three-minute rounds separated by two-minute breaks. Contestants had to wear international-style gloves and trunks and their feet were taped – to this day no shoes are worn. In spite of all these concessions to safety, today all surfaces of the body remain fair targets and any part of the body except the head may be used to strike an opponent. Common blows include high kicks to the neck, elbow thrusts to the face and head, knee hooks to the ribs and low kicks to the calf. Punching is considered the weakest of all blows, and kicking merely a way to 'soften up' one's opponent; knee and elbow strikes are decisive in most matches.

Phra Nakorn Bar & Gallery

BAR

32 MAP P56, C4

Located an ambivalent arm's length from the hype of Th Khao San, Phra Nakorn Bar and Gallery is a home away from hovel for Thai students and arty types, with eclectic decor and changing gallery exhibits. Our tip: head directly for the breezy rooftop and order some of the bar's cheap and tasty Thai food. (www.facebook.com/Phranakorn barandgallery; 58/2 Soi Damnoen Klang Tai; ⏰6pm-1am; 🚤klorng boat to Phanfa Leelard Pier)

Hippie de Bar

BAR

33 MAP P56, C3

Hippie boasts a funky retro vibe and indoor and outdoor seating, all set to the type of indie-pop soundtrack that you're unlikely to hear elsewhere in town. Despite being located on Th Khao San, there are surprisingly few foreign faces, so it's a great place to make some new Thai friends. (www.facebook.com/hippie.debar; 46 Th Khao San; ⏰3pm-2am; 🚤Phra Athit/Banglamphu Pier)

Lava Gold

CLUB

34 MAP P56, C3

Descend the stairs to this long-standing, perpetually packed, Th Khao San disco. The DJs are probably not going to win international acclaim, but that's the way the boozy crowd likes it. (www.facebook. com/Lava.Gold.Club; 249 Th Khao San; ⏰7pm-4am; 🚤Tha Phra Athit/Banglamphu)

Rolling Bar

BAR

35 MAP P56, E3

An escape from hectic Th Khao San is a good enough excuse to schlep to this quiet canalside boozer. Live music and salty bar snacks are reasons to stay. (Th Prachathipatai; ⏰5pm-midnight; 🚤klorng boat to Phanfa Leelard Pier)

Entertainment

Rajadamnern Stadium

SPECTATOR SPORT

36 MAP P56, H2

Rajadamnern Stadium, Bangkok's oldest and most venerable venue for *moo·ay tai* (Thai boxing; also spelt *muay Thai*), hosts matches on Monday, Wednesday and Thursday from 6.30pm to around 11pm, and Sunday at 3pm and 6.30pm. Be sure to buy tickets from the official ticket counter or online, not from the touts and scalpers who hang around outside the entrance. (สนามมวยราชดำเนิน; www.rajadamnern.com; off Th Ratchadamnoen Nok; tickets 3rd class/2nd class/ringside 1000/1500/2500B; ⏰Matches Mon-Thur from 6.30-11pm, Sun 3pm & 6.30pm; 🚤Thewet Pier, Ⓢ Phaya Thai exit 3 & taxi)

Brick Bar

LIVE MUSIC

This pub in the basement of Buddy Lodge (see 43 Map56, D3), one of our favourite destinations in Bangkok for live music, hosts a nightly revolving cast of bands for an almost exclusively Thai crowd – many of whom will end the night dancing on the tables. Brick Bar can get infamously packed, so be sure to get there early. (www.brickbarkhaosan.com; 265 Th Khao San; admission Sat & Sun 150B; ⏲7pm-1.30am; ⛴Phra Athit/ Banglamphu Pier)

Ad Here the 13th
LIVE MUSIC

37 ⭐ MAP P56, D1

This closet-sized blues bar is everything a neighbourhood joint should be: lots of regulars, cold beer and heart-warming tunes delivered by a masterful house band (starting at 10pm). Everyone knows each other, so don't be shy about mingling. (www.facebook.com/adhere13thbluesbar; 13 Th Samsen; ⏲6pm-midnight; ⛴Phra Athit/ Banglamphu Pier)

Brown Sugar
LIVE MUSIC

38 ⭐ MAP P56, F3

You'll find this long-standing live-music staple in a cavernous shophouse. The music, spanning from funk to jazz, starts at 8pm most nights and draws heaps of locals, particularly on weekends. (www.brownsugarbangkok.com; 469 Th Phra Sumen; ⏲5pm-1am Tue-Thu & Sun, to 2am Fri & Sat; ⛴klorng boat to Phanfa Leelard Pier, Phra Athit/ Banglamphu Pier)

jazz happens!
LIVE MUSIC

39 ⭐ MAP P56, B2

Linked with Silpakorn University, Thailand's most famous arts

Stall on Th Khao San (p61)

Sacred Shopping

The stretch of **Thanon Bamrung Meuang Religious Shops** (ถนน บำรุงเมือง; Map p57, F6; Th Bamrung Meuang; ⏰9am-6pm; 🚤klorng boat to Phanfa Leelard Pier) – one of Bangkok's oldest streets and originally an elephant path leading to the Grand Palace – from Th Mahachai to Th Tanao is lined with shops selling all manner of Buddhist religious paraphernalia. Behind the shopfronts, back-room workshops produce gigantic bronze Buddha images for wát all over Thailand. You probably don't need a Buddha statue or an eerily lifelike model of a famous monk, but looking is fun, and who knows when you might need to do a great deal of Thai-style merit making.

university, jazz happens! is a stage for aspiring musical talent. With four acts playing most nights and a huge selection of bar snacks, you'll be thoroughly entertained. (www.jazzhappens.org; 62 Th Phra Athit; ⏰7pm-1am; 📶; 🚤Phra Athit/ Banglamphu Pier)

Shopping

Thanon Khao San Market
GIFTS & SOUVENIRS

40 🅰 MAP P56, C3

The main guesthouse strip in Banglamphu is a day-and-night shopping bazaar peddling all the backpacker 'essentials': profane T-shirts, bootleg MP3s, hemp clothing, fake student ID cards, knock-off designer wear, selfie sticks, orange juice and, of course, those croaking wooden frogs. (Th Khao San; ⏰10am-midnight; 🚤Phra Athit/Banglamphu Pier)

Heritage Craft
ARTS & CRAFTS

41 🅰 MAP P56, C6

Handicrafts with a conscience: this new boutique is an atmospheric showcase for the quality domestic wares of **ThaiCraft** (www.thaicraft. org; L fl, Jasmine City Bldg, cnr Soi 23 & Th Sukhumvit; Ⓜ Sukhumvit exit 2, Ⓢ Asok exit 3), some of which are produced via fair-trade practices. Items include silks from Thailand's northeast, baskets from the south and jewellery from the north; there's also an inviting on-site cafe. (35 Th Bamrung Meuang; ⏰11am-6pm Mon-Fri; 🚤klorng boat to Phanfa Leelard Pier)

Mowaan
HEALTH & WELLBEING

42 🅰 MAP P56, D6

With nearly a century under its belt, this brand makes lozenges, inhalers, oils and balms rooted in Thai herbal medicine. Even if you are in satisfactory health, a visit to the immaculately preserved showroom is akin to a trip back in time. (www.mowaan.com/en; 9 Soi Thesa; ⏱9am-5pm; 🚤klorng boat to Phanfa Leelard Pier)

Lofty Bamboo ARTS & CRAFTS

43 🔒 MAP P56, D3

No time to make it to northern Thailand? No problem. At this shop you can get the type of colourful, hill-tribe-inspired clothes, cloth items and other handicrafts you'd find at the markets in Chiang Mai and Chiang Rai. And best of all, a purchase supports economic self-sufficiency in upcountry villages. (ground fl, Buddy Lodge, 265 Th Khao San; ⏱10.30am-8pm; 🚤Phra Athit/Banglamphu Pier)

Nittaya Thai Curry FOOD & DRINKS

44 🔒 MAP P56, C2

Follow your nose: Nittaya is famous throughout Thailand for her pungent, high-quality curry pastes. Pick up a couple of takeaway canisters for prospective dinner parties or peruse the snack and gift sections, where visitors to Bangkok load up on local specialities for friends and family back in the provinces. (136-40 Th Chakraphatdi Phong; ⏱9am-7pm Mon-Sat; 🚤Phra Athit/Banglamphu Pier)

Taekee Taekon ARTS & CRAFTS

45 🔒 MAP P56, B1

This atmospheric shop has a decent selection of Thai textiles from the country's main silk-producing areas, especially northern Thailand, as well as interesting postcards not widely available elsewhere. (118 Th Phra Athit; ⏱9am-5pm Mon-Sat; 🚤Phra Athit/Banglamphu Pier)

Top Sight 📷
Dusit Palace Park

*Following his first European tour in 1897, Rama
V (King Chulalongkorn; r 1868–1910) returned
with visions of European castles and set about
transforming these styles into a uniquely Thai
expression, today's Dusit Palace Park. These days
the king has yet another home and this complex
now holds a house museum and other cultural
collections.*

วังสวนดุสิต

bounded by Th Ratcha-
withi, Th U Thong Nai & Th
Nakhon Ratchasima

adult/child 100/20B, with
Grand Palace ticket free

🕙9.30am-4pm Tue-Sun

🚤Thewet Pier, S Phaya
Thai exit 2 & taxi

When we stopped by, Dusit Palace Park was temporarily closed for renovation and is expected to be open again in 2018; enquire at the ticket office of the Grand Palace.

Vimanmek Teak Mansion

Originally constructed on Ko Si Chang in 1868 and moved to the present site in 1910, this structure (pictured left) contains 81 rooms, halls and anterooms, and is said to be the world's largest golden-teak building, allegedly built without the use of a single nail. Compulsory tours (in English) leave every 30 minutes between 9.45am and 3.15pm, and last about an hour.

Ancient Cloth Museum

A beautiful collection of traditional silks and cottons that make up the royal cloth collection.

Abhisek Dusit Throne Hall

Originally built as a throne hall for Rama V in 1904, this building is typical of the finer architecture of the era. Victorian-influenced gingerbread architecture and Moorish porticoes blend to create a striking and distinctly Thai exterior.

Royal Thai Elephant Museum

Two large stables that once housed three white elephants – animals whose auspicious albinism automatically make them crown property – now form this museum.

★ Top Tips

o Admission to Dusit Palace Park is included with the Grand Palace ticket fee.

o Because Dusit Palace Park is royal property, visitors should wear long pants (no cropped pants) or long skirts and sleeved shirts.

✗ Take a Break

o If you find yourself at Dusit Palace Park at lunchtime, head to **Likhit Kai Yang** (off Th Ratchadamnoen Nok, no Roman-script sign; mains 50-300B; ⏲9am-9pm; ✳; S Phaya Thai exit 3 & taxi) for some of the city's best grilled chicken.

o If it's evening, get a craft beer or a boozy ice-cream coke at **Hazel's Ice Cream Parlor & Fine Drinks** (www.facebook.com/HazelsParlor; 171 Th Chakraphatdi Phong; ⏲5-11pm Tue-Sat, noon-11pm Sun; S Phaya Thai exit 3 & taxi).

CHINA TOWN SCALA

SHARK'S FIN - BIRD'S NEST

SEAFOOD

Hotel Royal
Bangkok • Chinatown

16

AVEL

Explore ⊕
Chinatown

Chinatown embodies everything that's hectic, noisy and polluted about Bangkok, but that's what makes it such a fascinating area to explore. The area's big sights – namely Wat Traimit (Golden Buddha) and the street markets – are worth hitting, but be sure to set aside enough time to do some map-free wandering among the neon-lit gold shops, hidden temples, crumbling shopfronts and pencil-thin alleys.

Get up early to beat the tour buses to the golden Buddha at Wat Traimit (p78). Cross the frenetic market alleyway that is Talat Mai (p84) to the mazelike Chinese-style temple, Wat Mangkon Kamalawat (p84). Make your way to Phahurat, Bangkok's Little India, and take lunch at Royal India (p89). Chinatown begins to pick up again in the early evening, and this is the best time to follow our food-centric walking tour (p80). After dinner, enjoy views of Mae Nam Chao Phraya from the rooftop bar at River Vibe (p91). Finish your evening at the nocturnal flower marketm Pak Khlong Talat.

Getting There & Around

Hua Lamphong, the closest MRT (Metro) station, is about a kilometre from many sights, so you'll have to take a longish walk or a short taxi ride. An alternative is to take the Chao Phraya Express Boat to the stop at Ratchawong Pier, from where it's a brief walk to most restaurants and a bit further to most sights.

Ⓜ **MRT** Hua Lamphong.

🚤 **Chao Phraya Express Boat** Marine Department Pier, Ratchawong Pier, Saphan Phut/Memorial Bridge Pier and Pak Klong Taladd Pier.

Neighbourhood Map on p82

Th Yaowarat, Chinatown's main street KRIANG KAN/SHUTTERSTOCK ©

Top Sight 🏛️
Wat Traimit (Golden Buddha)

Wat Traimit, also known as the Temple of the Golden Buddha, is home to the world's largest gold statue, a gleaming, 3m-tall, 5.5-tonne Buddha with a mysterious past. The image is thought to date from as long ago as the 13th century, but if it's possible for a Buddha image to live a double life, this one has done so.

◎ **MAP P82, G4**

วัดไตรมิตร, Temple of the Golden Buddha

Th Mittaphap Thai-China

admission 100B

🕐 8am-5pm

🚤 Ratchawong Pier,
Ⓜ Hua Lamphong exit 1

The Golden Buddha

The star attraction at Wat Traimit is the gold Buddha image. Located on the 4th floor of the temple compound's imposing marble structure, the gold statue was originally 'discovered' some 60 years ago beneath a stucco or plaster exterior when it fell from a crane while being moved. It's thought that the covering was added to protect the statue from marauding hordes, either during the late Sukhothai period or later in the Ayuthaya period when the city was under siege by the Burmese.

Phra Maha Mondop

In 2009 a new home for the Buddha statue was built. Combining marble, Chinese-style balustrades and a steep Thai-style roof, it's now one of the taller buildings in Chinatown, and the golden spire can be seen from blocks away. Surrounding the structure is a narrow strip of grass watered via mist fountains.

Yaowarat Chinatown Heritage Center

On the 3rd floor of Phra Maha Mondop is this small but engaging **museum** (ศูนย์ประวัติศาสตร์เยาวราช; 40B; ⊙8am-5pm Tue-Sun), which houses multimedia exhibits on Chinese immigration to Thailand, as well as on the history of Bangkok's Chinatown and its residents. Particularly fun are the miniature dioramas that depict important cultural facets of Thai-Chinese life.

Phra Buddha Maha Suwanna Patimakorn Exhibition

An extension of the Yaowarat Chinatown Heritage Center, this 2nd-floor **exhibition** (นิทรรศการพระพุทธมหาสุวรรณปฏิมากร; ⊙8am-5pm Tue-Sun) recounts how Wat Traimit's Buddha statue was made, discovered and came to arrive at its current home. If you've ever wondered how to make – or move – a 5.5-tonne gold Buddha statue, your questions will be answered here.

★ **Top Tips**

○ Wat Traimit is a short walk from the MRT stop at Hua Lamphong.

○ Don't overlook the two interesting museums – closed on Mondays – located in the same structure as the Golden Buddha.

✕ **Take a Break**

Located in the same compound, in an unsigned covered structure just east of the Buddha statue, unassuming Khun Yah Cuisine (p87) does excellent central Thai-style curry and noodle dishes. There's no menu; rather, just point to whatever looks tasty, and be sure to get there before noon.

Walking Tour 🥾

A Taste of Chinatown

Street food rules in Chinatown, making the area ideal for a culinary adventure. Although many vendors stay open late, the more popular stalls tend to sell out quickly, so the best time to feast in this area is from 7pm to 9pm. Don't attempt this walk on a Monday, when most of the city's street vendors stay at home. And note that many of the stalls don't have Roman-script signs.

Walk Facts

Start Nai Mong Hoi Thod; 🚤 Tha Ratchawong, Ⓜ Hua Lamphong exit & taxi

End Shanghai Terrace; 🚤 Tha Ratchawong, Ⓜ Hua Lamphong exit & taxi

Length 1.5km; two to three hours

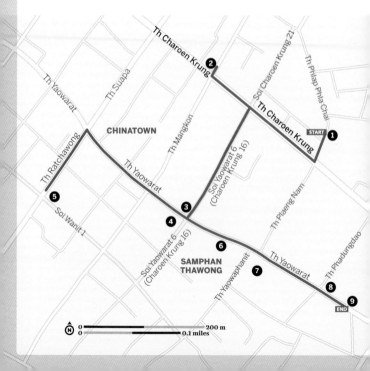

❶ Nai Mong Hoi Thod

Start at the intersection of Th Plaeng Nam and Th Charoen Krung. Head north along Th Phlap Phla Chai until you reach **Nai Mong Hoi Thod** (mains 50-70B; ◷5-10pm Tue-Sun), renowned for its delicious *hŏy tôrt* (mussels or oysters fried with egg and a sticky batter).

❷ Jék Pûi

Backtrack to Th Charoen Krung and turn right. At Th Mangkon make a right. To your left is a table-less **stall** (mains from 30B; ◷4-8pm Tue-Sun) renowned for its mild Chinese-style Thai curries.

❸ Gŏo·ay dĕe·o kôo·a gài

Cross Th Charoen Krung again, turn left, and head east to Soi 16 (aka Trok Itsaranuphap). At the end of this narrow market lane you'll see a gentleman making **gŏo·ay dĕe·o kôo·a gài** (Soi 6, Th Yaowarat; mains from 30B; ◷5-10pm Tue-Sun), wide rice noodles fried with chicken, egg and garlic oil.

❹ Nay Lék Ûan

Upon emerging at Th Yaowarat, cross over to the busy market area directly across the street. The first **vendor** (Soi Yaowarat 11; mains from 40B; ◷5pm-midnight) on the right sells *gŏo·ay jáp nám săi*, an intensely peppery broth containing rice noodles and pork offal.

❺ Phat Thai Ratchawong

Go west on Th Yaowarat. Turn left onto Th Ratchawong, where a **stall** (Th Ratchawong; mains from 30B; ◷7-11pm Tue-Sun) run by a Chinese-Thai couple, offers a unique version of *pàt tai* – Thailand's most famous dish – fried over coals and served in banana leaf cups.

❻ Mangkorn Khŏw

Backtrack along Th Yaowarat to the corner of Th Yaowaphanit, where you'll see a **street stall** (mains from 50B; ◷6pm-midnight Tue-Sun) selling tasty *bà·mèe*, Chinese-style wheat noodles served with crab or barbecued pork.

❼ Boo·a loy nám kĭng

Adjacent to Mangkorn Khŏw is a no-name stall that does Chinese-Thai desserts, including delicious **boo·a loy nám kĭng** (mains from 30B; ◷5-11pm Tue-Sun; ✍), dumplings stuffed with rich black sesame paste and served in a spicy ginger broth.

❽ Seafood Stalls

Cross Th Yaowarat and head east until you reach the intersection with Th Phadungdao; this corner is the unmistakable location of **Lek & Rut and T&K** (p89), two extremely popular and nearly identical open-air seafood stalls.

❾ Shanghai Terrace

Continue east along Th Yaowarat until you reach the Shanghai Mansion Hotel; on the 2nd floor you'll find **Shanghai Terrace** (ground fl, Shanghai Mansion, 479-481 Th Yaowarat; ◷6-11pm), a jazz bar that's a timely – and graciously air-conditioned – end to your walk.

A **B** **C** **D**

1

Saranrom Royal Garden

Rommaneenart Park

Soi Long Tha

Th Mahachai

Th Charoen Krung

⭐24

17 🍽

Old Siam Plaza

Th Burapha

Th Phahurat

Nakhon Kasem (Thieves' Market)

2

Th Ban Mo

Th Triphet

Phahurat 9 ⊙

Th Mahachai

Th Yaowarat

Th Maha Rat

⊙16

Th Chakkaraphet

6 ⊙ Sampeng Lane

Soi Wanit 1

Th Chakrawat

CHINATOWN

Atsadang 🍽 ⊙ Pier 🍽

5 ⊙ Pak Khlong Talat

Th Chakrawat

Th Ratchawong

3

Pak Klong Taladd Pier

Saphan Phut/ Memorial Bridge Pier

4 ⊙

Saphan Phut (Memorial Bridge)

🍽

Church of Santa Cruz

Phra Pokklao Bridge

Ratchawong 🍽 Pier

Th Ratchawong

Mae Nam Chao Phraya

4

Th Arun Amarin

Th Prachathipok

5

Th Din Daeng

Th Somdet Chao Phraya

6

For reviews see	
⊙ Top Sights	p78
⊙ Sights	p84
🍽 Eating	p86
🍺 Drinking	p89
⭐ Entertainment	p91

0 ————— 400 m
0 ————— 0.2 miles

A **B** **C** **D**

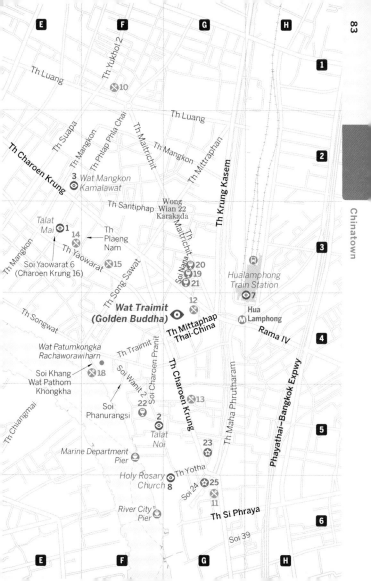

E
F
G
H

1
2
3
4
5
6

Th Luang
Th Yukhol 2
⊗10
Th Luang

Th Charoen Krung

Th Suapa
Th Mangkon
Th Phlap Phla Chai
Th Maitrichit
Th Mangkon
Th Mittraphan
Th Krung Kasem

3 Wat Mangkon
Kamalawat

Th Santiphap
Wong
Wian 22
Karakada

Th Maitrichit

Talat
Mai ⊙1
14
Th
Plaeng
Nam
Th Yaowarat ⊗15
Soi Yaowarat 6
(Charoen Krung 16)
Th Mangkon

Th Song Sawat

Soi Nana

⊗20
⊕19
⊕21

Hualamphong
Train Station
⊕7
Hua
Ⓜ Lamphong
Rama IV

Wat Traimit
(Golden Buddha) ⊙

12
⊗

Th Mittaphap
Thai-China

Th Songwat

Wat Patumkongka
Rachaworawiharn
Soi Khang
Wat Pathom
Khongkha
⊗18

Th Traimit

Soi Wanit 2

Soi Charoen Pranit

Soi
Phanurangsi

Th Charoen Krung

⊗13

Th Maha Phrutharam

Phayathai–Bangkok Expwy

Th Chiangmai

22
⊕
2
⊙
Talat
Noi

Marine Department
Pier ⊙

23
☆

Holy Rosary
Church 8 ⊙
Th Yotha
Soi 24

25
⊕
11
⊗

River City
Pier ⊙

Th Si Phraya

Soi 39

E
F
G
H

Sights

Talat Mai   MARKET

1 MAP P82, E3

With nearly two centuries of commerce under its belt, New Market is no longer an entirely accurate name for this strip of commerce. Regardless, this is Bangkok's, if not Thailand's, most Chinese market, and the dried goods, seasonings, spices and sauces will be familiar to anyone who's ever spent time in China. Even if you're not interested in food, the hectic atmosphere (be on guard for motorcycles squeezing between shoppers) and exotic sights and smells create something of a surreal sensory experience. (ตลาดใหม่; Soi Yaowarat 6/Charoen Krung 16; ☉6am-6pm; 🚢Ratchawong Pier, Ⓜ Hua Lamphong exit 1 & taxi)

Talat Noi   AREA

2 MAP P82, F5

This microcosm of soi life is named after a small *(nóy)* market *(dà·làht)*

Living on a Prayer

In many of Chinatown's temples, you'll see locals shaking cans of thin sticks called *see·am see*. You can also play: when a stick falls to the floor, look at its number and find the corresponding paper. It will give you a no-nonsense appraisal of your future in Thai, Chinese and English.

---

that sets up between Soi 22 and Soi 20, off Th Charoen Krung. Wandering here you'll find streamlike soi turning in on themselves, weaving through noodle shops, grease-stained machine shops and people's living rooms. (ตลาดน้อย; off Th Charoen Krung; ☉7am-7pm; 🚢Marine Department Pier)

Wat Mangkon Kamalawat   BUDDHIST TEMPLE

3 MAP P82, E2

Clouds of incense and the sounds of chanting form the backdrop at this Chinese-style Mahayana Buddhist temple. Surrounding the temple are vendors selling food for the gods – steamed lotus-shaped dumplings and oranges – which are donated to the temple in exchange for merit. Dating back to 1871, it's the largest and most important religious structure in the area, and during the annual **Vegetarian Festival** (☉Sep or Oct), religious and culinary activities are particularly active here. (วัดมังกร กมลาวาส; cnr Th Charoen Krung & Th Mangkon; admission free; ☉6am-6pm; 🚢Ratchawong Pier, Ⓜ Hua Lamphong exit 1 & taxi)

Church of Santa Cruz   CHURCH

4 MAP P82, A3

Centuries before Sukhumvit became Bangkok's international district, the Portuguese claimed *fa·ràng* (Western) supremacy on a riverside plot of land given to them by King Taksin in appreciation for their support after the fall of Ayuthaya. Located on this concession, the Church of Santa Cruz dates to 1913. (โบสถ์ซางตาครูส; Soi Kuti Jiin; ⏱7am-noon Sat & Sun; 🛥river-crossing ferry from Atsadang Pier)

Pak Khlong Talat
MARKET

5 ◎ MAP P82, B3

As of 2016, Bangkok's famous and formerly streetside flower market has been moved indoors. In the markets and shophouses that line Th Chakkaraphet, you'll still find piles of delicate orchids, rows of roses and stacks of button carnations, but the vibe isn't as exciting as it used to be. The best time to come is late at night, when the goods arrive from up-country. (ปากคลองตลาด, Flower Market; Th Chakkaraphet; ⏱24hr; 🛥Pak Klong Taladd Pier, Saphan Phut/Memorial Bridge Pier)

Sampeng Lane
MARKET

6 ◎ MAP P82, D2

Soi Wanit 1 – colloquially known as Sampeng Lane – is a narrow artery running parallel to Th Yaowarat and bisecting the commercial areas of Chinatown and Phahurat. The Chinatown portion of Sampeng Lane is lined with wholesale shops of hair accessories, pens, stickers, household wares and beeping, flashing knick-knacks. Near Th Chakrawat, gem and jewellery shops abound. Weekends are horribly crowded and it takes a gymnast's flexibility to squeeze past the pushcarts,

Waving the Yellow Flag

During the annual Vegetarian Festival in September/October, Bangkok's Chinatown becomes a virtual orgy of non-meat cuisine. The festivities centre on Chinatown's main street, Th Yaowarat, and the Talat Noi area, but food shops and stalls all over the city post yellow flags to announce their meat-free status.

motorcycles and other roadblocks. (สำเพ็ง; Soi Wanit 1; ⏱8am-6pm; 🛥Ratchawong Pier, Ⓜ Hua Lamphong exit 1 & taxi)

Hualamphong Train Station
HISTORIC BUILDING

7 ◎ MAP P82, H4

At the southeastern edge of Chinatown, Bangkok's main train station was built by Dutch architects and engineers between 1910 and 1916. (สถานีรถไฟหัวลำโพง; off Rama IV; Ⓜ Hua Lamphong exit 2)

Holy Rosary Church
CHURCH

8 ◎ MAP P82, G6

Portuguese seafarers were among the first Europeans to establish diplomatic ties with Siam, and their influence in the kingdom was rewarded with prime riverside real estate. When a Portuguese contingent moved across the river to the present-day Talat Noi area of Chinatown in 1787, they were

Street-Food Vendors' Day Off

Most of Bangkok's street-food vendors close up shop on Monday, so don't plan on eating in Chinatown – where much of the food is street based – on this day.

given this piece of land and built the Holy Rosary Church, known in Thai as Wat Kalawan, from the Portuguese 'Calvario' (Calvary). (วัดแม่พระลูกประคำกาลหว่าร์; cnr Th Yotha & Soi Charoen Phanit; ⊙Thai-language mass 7.30pm Mon-Sat, 8am, 10am & 7.30pm Sun; ⚓Marine Department Pier)

Phahurat   AREA

9 ◉ MAP P82, C2

Heaps of South Asian traders set up shop in Bangkok's small but bustling Little India, where everything from Bollywood movies to bindis is sold by enthusiastic, small-time traders. It's a great area to just wander through, stopping for masala chai and a Punjabi sweet as you go. The bulk of the action unfolds along unmarked Soi ATM, which runs alongside the large **India Emporium** (⊙10am-10pm) shopping centre. (พาหุรัด; Th Chakkaraphet; ⊙9am-5pm; ⚓Saphan Phut/Memorial Bridge Pier, Pak Klong Taladd Pier)

Eating

Nay Hong   STREET FOOD $

10 ⊗ MAP P82, F1

The reward for locating this hole-in-the-wall is one of Bangkok's best fried noodle dishes – gŏo·ay đĕe·o kôo·a gài (flat rice noodles fried with garlic oil, chicken and egg). No English-language menu. There's no English-language sign. To find Nay Hong, proceed north from the corner of Th Suapa and Th Luang, then turn right into the first side street; it's at the end of the narrow alleyway. (off Th Yukol 2; mains 35-50B; ⊙4-10pm; ⚓Ratch-awong Pier, Ⓜ Hua Lamphong exit 1 & taxi)

80/20   INTERNATIONAL $$

11 ⊗ MAP P82, G6

Don't call it fusion; rather, 80/20 excels at taking and blending Thai and Western ingredients and dishes, arriving at something altogether unique. The often savoury-leaning desserts, overseen by a Japanese pastry chef, are especially worth the trip. A progressive breath of air in otherwise conservative Chinatown. (✆02 639 1135; www.facebook.com/8020bkk; 1052-1054 Th Charoen Krung; mains from 240B; ⊙6pm-midnight Wed-Mon; ❄; ⚓Ratchawong Pier, Ⓜ Hua Lamphong exit 1)

Khun Yah Cuisine   THAI $

12 MAP P82, G4

Strategically located for a lunch break after visiting Wat Traimit (Golden Buddha), Khun Yah specialises in the full-flavoured curries, relishes, stir-fries and noodle dishes of central Thailand. Be sure to get here early, because come noon many dishes are already sold out.Khun Yah has no English-language sign (nor an English-language menu) but is located just east of the Golden Buddha, in the same compound. (off Th Mittaphap Thai-China, mains from 40B; 6am-1.30pm Mon-Fri; Ratchawong Pier, M Hua Lam-phong exit 1)

Fou de Joie   FRENCH $$

13 MAP P82, G5

Dining at the retro Hong Kong–themed Fou de Joie is like being an extra in a Wong Kar-Wai film. Better yet, the French-style crêpes and cheese platters – not to mention the upstairs barbecue – are more than just set pieces, and offer terrific value. (085 527 3511; 831 Soi 31, Th Charoen Krung; mains from 200B; 6pm-midnight Wed-Sun; ; Ratchawong Pier, M Hua Lamphong exit 1)

Hoon Kuang   CHINESE $$

14 MAP P82, E3

Serving the food of Chinatown's streets in air-con comfort is this low-key, long-standing staple. The must-eat dishes are pictured on

Outdoor dining, Th Yaowarat

ARTAPARTMENT/SHUTTERSTOCK ©

The Chinese Influence

In many ways Bangkok is a Chinese, as much as a Thai, city. The Chinese presence in Bangkok predates the founding of the city, when Thonburi Si Mahasamut was little more than a Chinese trading outpost on Mae Nam Chao Phraya. In the 1780s, during the construction of the new capital under Rama I (King Phraphutthayotfa; r 1782–1809), Hokkien, Teochew and Hakka Chinese were hired as labourers. Eventually these labourers and entrepreneurs were relocated to the districts of Yaowarat and Sampeng, today known as Bangkok's Chinatown.

Roots in Business

During the reign of Rama I, many Chinese began to gain status and wealth. They controlled many of Bangkok's shops and businesses and, because of increased trading ties with China, were responsible for an immense expansion in Thailand's market economy. Visiting Europeans during the 1820s were astonished by the number of Chinese trading ships on Mae Nam Chao Phraya, and some assumed that the Chinese formed the majority of Bangkok's population.

An Emerging Aristocracy

The newfound wealth of certain Chinese trading families created one of Thailand's first elite classes that was not directly related to royalty. Known as *jôw so·a*, these 'merchant lords' eventually obtained additional status by accepting official posts and royal titles, as well as by offering their daughters to the royal family. At one point, Rama V (King Chulalongkorn; r 1868–1910) took a Chinese consort. Today it is believed that more than half of the people in Bangkok can claim some Chinese ancestry.

Cultural Integration

During the reign of Rama III (King Phranangklao; r 1824–51), the Thai capital began to absorb many elements of Chinese food, design, fashion and literature. By the beginning of the 20th century, the ubiquity of Chinese culture, coupled with the tendency of the Chinese men to marry Thai women and assimilate into Thai culture, had resulted in relatively little difference between the Chinese and their Siamese counterparts.

the door, but it'd be a pity to miss the 'prawn curry flat rice noodle', a unique mash-up of two Chinese-Thai dishes – crab in curry powder and flash-fried noodles – that will make you wonder why they were ever served apart. (381 Th Yaowarat; mains 90-240B; ⏰11am-7.45pm Mon-Sat; ❄; 🛥Ratchawong Pier, Ⓜ Hua Lamphong exit 1 & taxi)

Thanon Phadungdao Seafood Stalls   STREET FOOD $$

15 ❌ MAP P82, F3

After sunset, these two opposing open-air restaurants – each of which claims to be the original – become a culinary train wreck of outdoor barbecues, screaming staff, iced seafood trays and messy pavement seating. True, the vast majority of diners are foreign tourists, but this has little impact on the cheerful setting, the fun experience and the cheap bill. (cnr Th Phadungdao & Th Yaowarat; mains 100-600B; ⏰4pm-midnight Tue-Sun; 🛥Ratchawong Pier, Ⓜ Hua Lamphong exit 1 & taxi)

Royal India   INDIAN $$

16 ❌ MAP P82, C2

Yes, we're aware that this hole-in-the-wall has been in every edition of our guide since the beginning, but after all these years it's still the most reliable place to eat in Little India. Try any of the delicious breads or rich curries, and don't forget to finish with a homemade Punjabi sweet. (392/1 Th Chakkaraphet; mains 135-220B; ⏰10am-10pm;

❄; 🖊; 🛥Saphan Phut/Memorial Bridge Pier, Pak Klong Taladd Pier)

Old Siam Plaza   SWEETS $

17 ❌ MAP P82, C2

Sugar junkies, be sure to stop here. The ground floor of this shopping centre is a candyland of traditional Thai sweets and snacks, most made right before your eyes. (cnr Th Phahurat & Th Triphet; mains 30-90B; ⏰10am-7pm; ❄; 🛥Saphan Phut/Memorial Bridge Pier, Pak Klong Taladd Pier)

Samsara   JAPANESE, THAI $$

18 ❌ MAP P82, F4

Combining Japanese and Thai dishes, Belgian beers and an artfully ramshackle atmosphere, Samsara is one of Chinatown's most eclectic places to eat. Its food is also tasty, and the generous riverside breezes and views simply add to the package. The restaurant is at the end of tiny Soi Khang Wat Pathum Khongkha, just west of the temple of the same name. (Soi Khang Wat Pathum Khongkha; mains 110-320B; ⏰4pm-midnight Tue-Thu, to 1am Fri-Sun; 🖊; 🛥Ratchawong Pier, Ⓜ Hua Lamphong exit 1 & taxi)

Drinking

Tep Bar   BAR

19 🍺 MAP P82, G3

We never expected to find a bar this sophisticated – yet this fun – in Chinatown. Tep does it with a Thai-tinged, contemporary interior, tasty signature cocktails, Thai drinking snacks and raucous live Thai music performances from Thursday to Sunday. (www.facebook.com/tepbar; 69-71 Soi Nana; ⏰5pm-midnight Tue-Sun; Ⓜ Hua Lamphong exit 1)

Ba Hao BAR

20 🚇 MAP P82, G3

At this point, there's little original about this retro Chinese-themed refurbished shophouse on Soi Nana, but potable craft beer, inventive cocktails and really excellent Chinese-style bar snacks make Ba Hao stand out. Don't miss the Chinese pancake with braised pork belly, herbs and fried egg. (www.ba-hao.com; 8 Soi Nana; ⏰6pm-midnight Tue-Sun; ⛴Ratchawong Pier, Ⓜ Hua Lamphong exit 1)

Pijiu Bar BAR

Old West meets old Shanghai at this new yet classic-feeling bar near Ba Ho (see 20 🚇 Map p82, G3) The emphasis here is on beer ('pijiu' is Chinese for beer), with four revolving craft brews on tap, but perhaps even more enticing are the charcuterie platters (300B) that unite a variety of smoked and preserved meats from some of the best vendors in Chinatown. (www.facebook.com/pijiubar; 16 Soi Nana; ⏰5pm-midnight Tue-Sun; ⛴Ratchawong Pier, Ⓜ Hua Lamphong exit 1)

Teens of Thailand BAR

Probably the edgiest of the new bars in Chinatown's Soi Nana (see 19 🚇 Map p82, G3). Squeeze through the tiny wooden door of this refurbished shophouse to

Performing *kŏhn*, a traditional Thai dance-drama at Sala Chalermkrung

emerge at an artsy warehouse-like interior, with hipster barkeeps serving creative gin-based drinks, and an upright piano we're guessing doesn't get too much play time. (76 Soi Nana; ⏰7pm-midnight Tue-Sun; Ⓜ Hua Lamphong exit 1)

El Chiringuito BAR

21 ⭐ MAP P82, G3

Come to this retro-feeling bar for sangria, Spanish gin and bar snacks, or the revolving art exhibitions. Opening hours can be sporadic, so call or check the Facebook page before heading out. (📞086 340 4791; www.facebook.com/elchiringuitobangkok; 221 Soi Nana; ⏰6pm-midnight Thu-Sun; Ⓜ Hua Lamphong exit 1)

River Vibe BAR

22 ⭐ MAP P82, F5

Can't afford the overpriced cocktails at Bangkok's upscale rooftop bars? The excellent river views from the top of this guesthouse will hardly feel like a compromise. We suggest getting dinner elsewhere, though. (8th fl, River View Guesthouse, off Soi Charoen Phanit; ⏰7.30-11pm; 🚢Marine Department Pier, Ⓜ Hua Lamphong exit 1)

Entertainment

SoulBar LIVE MUSIC

23 ⭐ MAP P82, G5

An unlikely venue – and neighbourhood – for live music, this converted shophouse nonetheless plays host to live blues, jazz and soul from 9pm just about every night. (www.facebook.com/livesoulbarbangkok; 945 Th Charoen Krung; ⏰7pm-midnight Tue-Sun; 🚢Marine Department Pier, Ⓜ Hua Lamphong exit 1)

Sala Chalermkrung THEATRE

24 ⭐ MAP P82, C1

This art deco Bangkok landmark, a former cinema dating to 1933, is one of the few remaining places *kŏhn* (masked dance-drama based on stories from the *Ramakian*, the Thai version of the Indian epic *Ramayana*) can be witnessed. The traditional dance-drama is enhanced here by laser graphics, high-tech audio and English subtitles. Concerts and other events are also held; check the website for details. (📞02 224 4499; www.salachalermkrung.com; 66 Th Charoen Krung; tickets 800-1200B; ⏰shows 7.30pm Thu & Fri; 🚢Saphan Phut/Memorial Bridge Pier, Ⓜ Hua Lamphong exit 1 & taxi)

Soy Sauce Factory ARTS CENTRE

25 ⭐ MAP P82, G6

A former soy-sauce factory turned gallery/event space/bar/photo studio... Whatever it is, check the Facebook page to see what's currently on at this artsy, open-ended gathering place, indicative of the kind of changes currently underfoot in Bangkok's Chinatown. (www.facebook.com/soysaucefactory; Soi 24, Th Charoen Krung; ⏰10am-7pm Tue-Sun; Ⓜ Hua Lamphong exit 1)

Walking Tour 🥾

Chinatown's Back Lanes

*Pencil-thin back lanes, seemingly abandoned
shrines, concealed mansions and forgotten
neighbourhoods come in spades in this riverside
stretch of Bangkok's Chinatown.*

Walk Facts

Start Holy Rosary Church;
🚤 Tha Si Phraya/River
City

End Tha Ratchawong;
🚤 Tha Ratchawong

Length 3km; two to three
hours

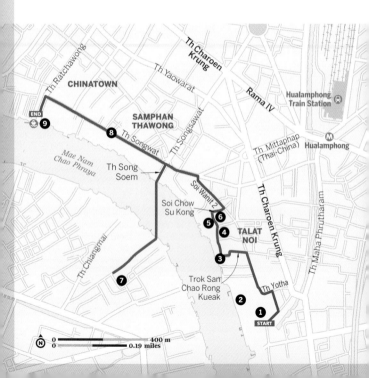

❶ Holy Rosary Church

Start your walk at **Holy Rosary Church**, originally located on a plot of land donated to Portuguese Catholics in 1787. Known in Thai as Wat Kalawan, from the Portuguese 'Calvario' (Calvary), the site of Jesus's crucifixion, the current structure dates to 1898.

❷ Siam Commercial Bank

Head north along Th Wanit 2; the next compound is the **Siam Commercial Bank**, the country's first domestic bank, dating back to 1910.

❸ San Chao Rong Kueak

Head past the Marine Department and turn left on Trok San Chao Rong Kueak; at the end of this lane is the eponymous **Chinese shrine**, a secluded spot for great river views.

❹ Jao Sua Son's Mansion

Continue along the riverfront path. Turn left at the first intersection and head north. On your right is the Chinese-style walled **compound of Jao Sua Son**, a former Chinese 'merchant lord'. Today the mansion is used as a diving school.

❺ San Jao Sien Khong

Continue north, passing the immense banyan tree. Turn left at the next intersection and follow the path towards the river; this will lead you to **San Jao Sien Khong**, a large Chinese shrine that is mostly quiet save for the annual Vegetarian Festival.

❻ Talat Noi

Exit the shrine on the north side, turning right on Soi Chow Su Kong, then left on Soi Wanit 2; you're now in the thick of the shophouses and garages of **Talat Noi** (ตลาดน้อย; Map p82, F5; off Th Charoen Krung; ⏰7am-7pm; 🚢Marine Department Pier).

❼ Tha Wat Thong Thammachat

Turn right on Th Phanurangsi, then turn left on Th Songwat. Head north briefly, then turn left on Th Song Soem; at the end of this lane is a tiny, unmarked pier. Take the river-crossing ferry (5B, from 5am to 9pm) to **Tha Wat Thong Thammachat**, just west of where you'll find a semi-enclosed compound of Chinese-style shophouses.

❽ Th Songwat

Return to the Bangkok side and head west along the crumbling riverside warehouses and shophouses of **Th Songwat**.

❾ Ratchawong Pier

Turn left on Th Ratchawong, where you'll reach the street's eponymous **pier**, and the end of your walk.

Explore ✦

Siam Square, Pratunam, Phloen Chit & Ratchathewi

Multistorey malls and never-ending markets leave no doubt that Siam Square, Pratunam and Phloen Chit combine to form Bangkok's commercial district. If you're serious about shopping, set aside the better part of a day to burn your baht here. Ratchathewi is where you can check out a more suburban side of Bangkok.

Be sure to take in the architecture of Jim Thompson House (p96). Cross over to the seven storeys of commerce that is MBK Center (p111) and have a tasty lunch at MBK Food Island (p103). Follow the elevated Sky Walk to the Erawan Shrine (p102), stopping along the way at various shopping centres (p111, p112) for even more retail therapy. For dinner, contrast your food-court lunch with a fancy feast at Gaa (p104) or a nouveau-Thai at Sra Bua by Kiin Kiin (p107).

Getting There & Around

The BTS (Skytrain) interchange at Siam has also made this bustling area the centre of modern Bangkok. Only a few blocks away, the attractions of Ratchathewi are all within walking distance of the BTS stop at Victory Monument and can be covered in a couple of hours.

S **BTS** To Siam Sq, Pratunam and Phloen Chit: Siam, National Stadium, Chit Lom, Phloen Chit and Ratchadamri. To Ratchathewi: Ratchathewi, Phaya Thai and Victory Monument.

🛶 **Canal boat** To Siam Sq, Pratunam and Phloen Chit: Sapan Hua Chang Pier, Pratunam Pier and Wireless Pier. To Ratchathewi: Pratunam Pier.

Neighbourhood Map on p98

Siam Discovery (p111) I VIEWFINDER/SHUTTERSTOCK ©

Top Sight 📷
Jim Thompson House

In 1959, 12 years after he single-handedly turned Thai silk into a hugely successful export business, American Jim Thompson bought a piece of land next to Khlong Saen Saeb and built himself a house. It wasn't, however, any old house. Thompson's love of all things Thai saw him buy six traditional wooden homes and reconstruct them in his garden.

◎ MAP P98, A2

เรือนไทยจิมทอมป์สัน

www.jimthompsonhouse.com

6 Soi Kasem San 2

adult/student 150/100B

🕘 9am-6pm, compulsory tours every 20min

🚤 klorng boat to Sapan Hua Chang Pier, S National Stadium exit 1

The House

Thompson adapted the six Thai structures to create a larger home in which each room had a more familiar Western function. Another departure from tradition is the way Thompson arranged each wall with its exterior side facing the house's interior. Some of the homes were brought from the old royal capital of Ayuthaya; others were pulled down and floated across the canal.

Thompson's Art Collection

Thompson's small but splendid Asian art collection is also on display in the main house: pieces include rare Chinese porcelain and Burmese, Cambodian and Thai artefacts. Thompson had a particularly astute eye for somewhat less flashy but nonetheless charming objects, such as the 19th-century mouse maze that resembles a home.

The Grounds

After the tour, be sure to poke around the house's jungle-like gardens, which include ponds filled with exotic fish. The compound also includes a cafe/restaurant and a shop flogging Jim Thompson–branded silk goods.

Jim Thompson Art Center

The compound also includes the **Jim Thompson Art Center** (⏱9am-8pm), a museum with revolving displays spanning a variety of media; recent exhibitions have seen contributions from the likes of Palme d'Or-winning Thai film-maker, Apichatpong Weerasethakul.

Read more about Jim Thompson on p101.

★ Top Tips

○ Beware of well-dressed touts in the soi near the Jim Thompson House who will tell you it is closed and then try to haul you off on a dodgy buying spree.

○ The house can only be viewed via a guided tour, which is available in Chinese, English, French, Japanese and Thai.

○ Photography is not allowed inside any of the buildings.

✗ Take a Break

The compound is home to the **Thompson Bar & Restaurant** (www.jimthompsonrestaurant.com; mains 160-480B; ⏱11am-5pm & 6-10pm; ❄ ☂ ; **S** National Stadium exit 2), which serves somewhat gentrified Thai food. Alternatively, head over to MBK Food Island (p103), one of the city's best food courts, for cheap Thai eats.

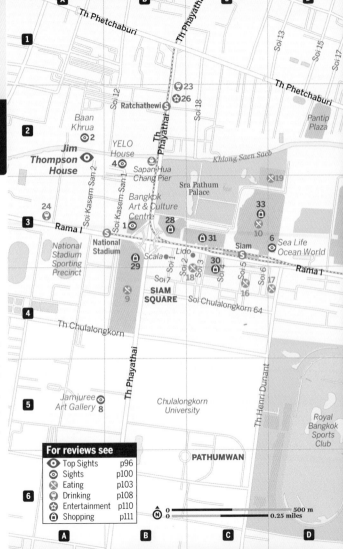

A B C D

1

Th Phetchaburi

Th Phayathai

Soi 13
Soi 15
Soi 17

Th Phetchaburi

Soi 12

⊗ 23
★ 26

Ratchathewi Ⓢ

Soi 18

Pantip
Plaza

2

Baan
Khrua

◉ 2

Jim
Thompson
House ◉

YELO
House

◉ 4

Khlong Saen Saeb

Sapan Hua
Chang Pier

Sra Pathum
Palace

⊗ 19

24
◉

Bangkok
Art & Culture
Centre

33
🔒

3

Rama 1

◉ 1 Ⓢ

National
Stadium

28
🔒

⊗ 10 6 ◎

🔒 31

Siam
Ⓢ

Sea Life
Ocean World

National
Stadium
Sporting
Precinct

🔒 29

Scala ●

Soi 2

Lido

30
🔒

Soi 5

Soi 4

Rama 1

Soi 1

⊗ 3
⊗ 18

Soi 6

17 ⊗

4

Th Chulalongkorn

⊗ 9

**SIAM
SQUARE**

Soi 7

Soi Chulalongkorn 64

⊗ 16

Soi Kasem San 2

Soi Kasem San 1

Th Phayathai

Th Phayathai

Th Henri Dunant

5

Jamjuree
Art Gallery ◉ 8

Chulalongkorn
University

Royal
Bangkok
Sports
Club

PATHUMWAN

For reviews see	
◉ Top Sights	p96
◎ Sights	p100
⊗ Eating	p103
⊙ Drinking	p108
★ Entertainment	p110
🔒 Shopping	p111

Ⓝ 0 _____ 500 m
0 _____ 0.25 miles

A B C D

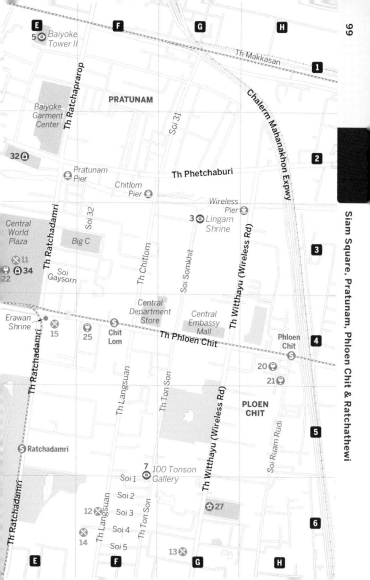

E
5 Baiyoke Tower II

F

G
Th Makkasan

H

1

Th Ratchaprarop

PRATUNAM

Chalerm Mahanakhon Expwy

Baiyoke Garment Center

Soi 31

2
32

Pratunam Pier

Chitlom Pier

Th Phetchaburi

Wireless Pier

3 Lingam Shrine

Th Ratchadamri

Soi 32

Central World Plaza

11
22 34

Big C

Soi Gaysorn

Th Chitlom

Soi Somkhit

Th Witthayu (Wireless Rd)

3

Central Department Store

Central Embassy Mall

Erawan Shrine

15

25

Chit Lom

Th Phloen Chit

Phloen Chit

4

20

21

Th Ratchadamri

Th Langsuan

Th Ton Son

PLOEN CHIT

Th Witthayu (Wireless Rd)

Soi Ruam Rudi

5

Ratchadamri

7 100 Tonson Gallery

Soi 1

12

Soi 2

Soi 3

Th Ton Son

27

14

Soi 4

Soi 5

13

E

F

G

H

6

Sights

Bangkok Art & Culture Centre

GALLERY

1  MAP P98, B3

This large, modern building in the centre of Bangkok has become one of the more significant players in the city's contemporary arts scene. As well as its three floors and 3000 sq metres of gallery space, the centre also contains shops, private galleries, cafes and an art library. Visit the website to see what exhibitions are on when you're in town. (BACC; หอศิลปวัฒนธรรมแห่งกรุงเทพมหานคร; www.bacc.or.th; cnr Th Phayathai & Rama I; admission free; ⏰10am-9pm Tue-Sat; ⓈNational Stadium exit 3)

Baan Khrua

AREA

2  MAP P98, A2

This canalside neighbourhood dates back to the turbulent years at the end of the 18th century, when Cham Muslims from Cambodia and Vietnam fought on the side of the new Thai king and were rewarded with this plot of land east of the new capital. The immigrants brought their silk-weaving traditions with them, and the community grew when the residents built Khlong Saen Saeb to better connect them to the river. (บ้านครัว; 🚣klorng boat to Sapan Hua Chang Pier, ⓈRatchathewi exit 1, National Stadium exit 1)

Bangkok Art & Culture Centre

Jim Thompson, the Man

Born in Delaware, USA, in 1906, Jim Thompson served in CIA's forerunner in Thailand during WWII. When in 1947 he spotted some silk in a market and was told it was woven in Baan Khrua, he found the only place in Bangkok where silk was still woven by hand.

Thompson's Thai silk eventually attracted the interest of fashion houses in New York, Milan, London and Paris, and he gradually built a worldwide clientele for a craft that had, just a few years before, been in danger of dying out.

By 1967 Thai silk had annual sales of almost US$1.5 million. In March that year Thompson went missing while out for an afternoon walk in the Cameron Highlands of western Malaysia; his business success, spy background and the fact that his sister was murdered in the same year made it an international mystery. Thompson has never been heard from since, but the conspiracy theories have never stopped. Was it communist spies? Business rivals? A hungry tiger? Although the mystery has never been solved, evidence revealed by American journalist Joshua Kurlantzick in his profile of Thompson, The Ideal Man, suggests that the vocal anti-American stance Thompson took later in his life may have made him a potential target of suppression by the CIA.

Lingam Shrine
MONUMENT

3 ◉ MAP P98, G3

Every village-neighbourhood has a local shrine. But it isn't every day you see a phallus garden like this lingam shrine, tucked back behind the staff quarters of the Swissôtel Nai Lert Park.When facing the entrance of the hotel, follow the small concrete pathway to the right, which winds down into the building beside the car park. The shrine is at the end of the building next to the *klorng*. (ศาลเจ้าแม่ทับทิม; Swissôtel Nai Lert Park, Th Witthayu/Wireless Rd; admission free; ◷24hr; ⛴klorng boat to Wireless Pier, Ⓢ Phloen Chit exit 1)

YELO House
GALLERY

4 ◉ MAP P98, B2

An art gallery? Vintage-clothing market? Co-working space? Cafe/restaurant? YELO House is so cool, it's hard to pin down what it actually is. So we'll go with the website's claim that it's a multifunction space for creative people. In practical terms, this means it's a place to dig through vintage clothes and ceramics, check out the latest exhibition, or enjoy an espresso in the canalside cafe. (www.yelohouse.com; 20/2 Soi Kasem San 1; ◷11am-8pm Tue-Sun)

Visiting the Erawan Shrine

One of the more clichéd tourist images of Bangkok is that of classical Thai dancers performing at the Hindu **shrine** (ศาลพระพรหม; Map p99, E4; cnr Th Ratchadamri & Th Phloen Chit; admission free; ⏰6am–11pm; Ⓢ Chit Lom exit 8) in front of the Grand Hyatt Erawan hotel. As with many things in Thailand, there is a great deal hidden behind this serene facade.

Thaksin's Downfall
After 50 years of largely benign existence, the Erawan Shrine became a point of focus when on 21 March 2006, a man destroyed the shrine with a hammer. The incident became a galvanising omen for the protest movement opposing then Prime Minister Thaksin Shinawatra. At a rally the following day, a protest leader suggested that Thaksin had masterminded the shrine's destruction in order to replace it with a 'dark force'. A new statue was installed, Thaksin was ousted in a coup in 2006 and has remained in exile since 2008.

Red Shirts
In 2010, the Ratchaprasong Intersection, where the shrine is located, became the main gathering point for antigovernment protesters wearing red. Images of the working-class rural protesters camped out in front of luxury shopfronts became a media staple. When the 'Red Shirts' were forcibly cleared out by the military on 19 May, five people were killed.

'Shutdown Bangkok' Protests
Three years later, Ratchaprasong Intersection yet again became a protest site, this time occupied by opponents of Thaksin's sister, then Prime Minister Yingluck Shinawatra. This time media images of the middle- and upper-class urban protesters in front of chic malls drew comparisons rather than contrasts. On 20 May 2014, the Royal Thai Army took over the government, leading the protesters to disperse.

An Act of Terrorism
The most significant event in the shrine's history came on the evening of 17 August 2015, when a bomb planted in the shrine compound exploded, killing 20 and injuring more than 120 people. Two suspects have been arrested, although their motives remain unclear and a verdict has yet to be reached.

Baiyoke Tower II   NOTABLE BUILDING

5 ⊙ MAP P98, E1

Cheesiness and altitude run in equal parts at Baiyoke Tower II, Bangkok's tallest building (to be usurped by a supertower slated to be finished in 2021). Ascend through a corridor decked with aliens and planets (and the *Star Wars* theme song) to emerge at the 84th-floor, open-air revolving platform that looks over a city whose concrete sprawl can appear never-ending. (ตึกใบหยก ๒; 22 Th Ratchaprarop; 300B; ⊙9am-11pm; 🛥klorng boat to Pratunam Pier)

Sea Life Ocean World   AQUARIUM

6 ⊙ MAP P98, D3

More than 400 species of fish, crustaceans and even penguins populate this vast underground facility. Diving with sharks (for a fee) is also an option if you have your diving licence, and there are shark and penguin feedings, although note that animal-welfare groups suggest that interaction with animals held in captivity creates stress for these creatures. (www.sealifebangkok.com; basement, Siam Paragon, 991/1 Rama I; adult/child from 490/350B; ⊙10am-9pm; ⓢSiam exits 3 & 5)

100 Tonson Gallery   GALLERY

7 ⊙ MAP P98, F5

Housed in a spacious residential villa and generally regarded as one of the city's top commercial galleries,

100 Tonson hosts a variety of contemporary exhibitions of all genres by local and international artists. (www.100tonsongallery.com; 100 Ton Son; admission free; ⊙11am-7pm Thu-Sun; ⓢChit Lom exit 4)

Jamjuree Art Gallery   GALLERY

8 ⊙ MAP P98, A5

This gallery, part of Chulalongkorn University's Faculty of Arts, emphasises modern spiritual themes and brilliantly coloured abstracts from emerging student artists. (หอศิลป์ จามจุรี; www.chamchuriartgallery.chula. ac.th; Jamjuree Bldg, Chulalongkorn University, Th Phayathai; admission free; ⊙10am-7pm Mon-Fri, 11am-6pm Sat & Sun; ⓢSiam exit 2 & taxi)

Eating

MBK Food Island   THAI $

9 ⊗ MAP P98, B4

With dozens of vendors offering exceedingly cheap and tasty regional Thai, international and even vegetarian dishes, MBK Food Island fiercely clings to its crown as the grandaddy of Bangkok food courts. (6th fl, MBK Center, cnr Rama I & Th Phayathai; mains 35-150B; ⊙10am-9pm; ❄🖉; ⓢNational Stadium exit 4)

Nuer Koo   CHINESE $

10 ⊗ MAP P98, C3

Is this the future of the noodle stall? Mall-bound Nuer Koo does a luxe version of the formerly humble bowl of beef noodles. Choose your cut of beef (including Kobe beef from Japan), enjoy the rich broth and cool air-con, and quickly forget about the good old days. (4th fl, Siam Paragon, 991/1 Rama I; mains 85-970B; ⏱11.30am-9.15pm; ❄; S Siam exits 3 & 5)

Din Tai Fung   CHINESE $$

11 🍴 MAP P98, E3

Most come to this lauded Taiwanese chain for the *xiao long bao* (broth-filled 'soup' dumplings). And so should you. But the other northern Chinese–style dishes are just as good, and justify exploring the more remote regions of the menu. (7th fl, CentralWorld, Th Ratchadamri; mains 65-350B;

Thai-style beef noodle soup

MAN OF STOCKER CITY/SHUTTERSTOCK ©

⏱11am-10pm; ❄🍴; S Chit Lom exit 9 to Sky Walk, Siam exit 6 to Sky Walk)

Gaa   INTERNATIONAL $$$

12 🍴 MAP P98, F6

A bright yellow and pink shophouse opposite Gaggan (p106) has been taken over by Gaggan's former sous chef, Garima Arora, who also honed her craft at Copenhagen's famed Noma. Classic Indian and Thai dishes are the specialities here, upgraded with modern cooking techniques and presented in artful 8–12-course tasting menus. Reservations are strongly recommended. (📞091 419 2424; www.gaabkk.com; 68/4 Soi Langsuan; set menu 1800-2400B; ⏱6-9.30pm; ❄; S Ratchadamri)

Saneh Jaan   THAI $$$

13 🍴 MAP P98, G6

A new restaurant with an old-school feel, Saneh Jaan features a menu of intriguing, unusual – and delicious – Thai dishes, many with a southern Thai accent. The prices reflect the semiformal vibe of the dining room, but portions are generous. (📞02 650 9880; www.facebook.com/sanehjaan; Glasshouse at Sindhorn, 130-132 Th Witthayu/Wireless Rd; set lunch 690B, mains 320-780B; ⏱11.30am-2pm & 6-10pm)

Cuisines of Bangkok

Geography, the influence of the royal palace and the Chinese and Muslim minorities have all pitched in to shape the local cuisine.

Central Thai Cuisine

The people of central Thailand are fond of sweet-savoury flavours, and many dishes include freshwater fish, pork, coconut milk and palm sugar. Central Thai eateries, particularly those in Bangkok, also serve a wide variety of seafood. Classic central Thai dishes include *yam lah dùk foo* (fried shredded catfish, chilli and peanuts served with a sweet-tart mango dressing) and *gaang sôm* (seafood, vegetables and/or herbs in a thick, tart broth).

Royal Thai Cuisine

A key influence on the city's kitchens has been the Bangkok-based royal court, which has been producing refined takes on central Thai dishes for nearly 300 years. Although previously available only within the palace walls, these so-called 'royal' Thai dishes can now be found across the city. One enduring example of royal cuisine is *mèe gròrp*, crispy noodles made the traditional way with a sweet-sour dressing.

Chinese-Thai Cuisine

Immigrants from southern China probably introduced the wok and several varieties of noodle dishes to Thailand. They also influenced Bangkok's cuisine in other ways: beef is not widely eaten in Bangkok due to a Chinese-Buddhist teaching that forbids eating 'large' animals. Perhaps the most common example of Thai-Chinese food is *kôw man gài*, Hainanese-style chicken rice.

Muslim-Thai Cuisine

Muslims are thought to have first visited Thailand during the late 14th century. They brought with them a cuisine based on meat and dried spices. Some Muslim dishes, such as *roh·đee*, a fried bread similar to the Indian *paratha*, have changed little, if at all. Others, such as the rich curry *gaang mát·sà·màn* are a unique blend of Thai and Indian/Middle Eastern cooking styles and ingredients.

Dining on the Cheap

The mall-based food courts in this part of town are cheap, clean, boast English-language menus and are increasingly stylish and inviting. Our favourites:

MBK Food Island (p103) The biggest and best.

Eathai (www.facebook.com/EathaibyCentral; basement, Central Embassy Mall, 1031 Th Phloen Chit; mains 60-360B; ⏱10am-10pm; ❄ 🍴 ; Ⓢ Phloen Chit exit 5) Here you'll find branches of several 'famous' stalls and restaurants.

Food Republic (4th fl, Siam Center, cnr Rama I & Th Phayathai; mains 30-200B; ⏱10am-10pm; ❄ 🍴 ; Ⓢ Siam exit 1) Located in Siam Center (p112), this is probably Bangkok's most attractive food court.

FoodPark (4th fl, Big C, 97/11 Th Ratchadamri; mains 30-90B; ⏱9am-9pm; ❄ ; Ⓢ Chit Lom exit 9 to Sky Walk) A Thai food court for Thais.

Gaggan
INDIAN $$$

14 ❌ MAP P98, F6

The white, refurbished villa that houses Gaggan seems more appropriate for an English-themed tea-house than a restaurant serving self-proclaimed 'progressive Indian cuisine', but Gaggan is all about incongruity. The set menus here span up to 10 courses, ranging from the daring (a ball of raita) to the traditional (some excellent tandoori), with bright flavours and unexpected but satisfying twists. Reservations essential. (📞02 652 1700; www.eatatgaggan.com; 68/1 Th Langsuan; set menu 5000B; ⏱6-11pm; ❄ 🍴 ; Ⓢ Ratchadamri exit 2)

Erawan Tea Room
THAI $$

15 ❌ MAP P98, E4

The oversized chairs, panoramic windows and variety of hot drinks make this one of Bangkok's best places to catch up with the paper. The lengthy menu of Thai standards will likely encourage you to linger a bit longer, and the selection of jams and teas to take away allows you to recreate the experience at home. (2nd fl, Erawan Bangkok, 494 Th Phloen Chit; mains 180-640B; ⏱10am-10pm; ❄ 🍴 ; Ⓢ Chit Lom exit 8)

Somtam Nua
THAI $

16 ❌ MAP P98, C4

It can't compete with the street stalls for flavour and authenticity, but if you need to be seen, particularly while in air-con and trendy surroundings, this is a good place to sample northeastern Thai specialities. Expect a line at dinner. (392/14 Soi 5, Siam Sq; mains 75-120B; ⏰10.45am-9.30pm; ❄ S Siam exit 4)

Coca Suki
CHINESE, THAI $$

17 MAP P98, D4

Immensely popular with Thai families, *sù·gêe* takes the form of a bubbling hotpot of broth and the raw ingredients to dip therein. Coca is one of the oldest purveyors of the dish, and this branch reflects the brand's efforts to appear more modern. Insider tip for fans of spice: be sure to request the tangy *tom yam* broth. (416/3-8 Th Henri Dunant; mains 100-800B; ⏰11am-11pm; ❄ S Siam exit 6)

Koko
THAI $$

18 MAP P98, C4

Perfect for omnivores and vegetarians alike, this casual cafe-like restaurant offers a lengthy vegie menu, not to mention a short but solid repertoire of meat-based Thai dishes, such as a Penang curry served with tender pork, or fish deep-fried and served with Thai herbs. (262/2 Soi 3, Siam Sq; mains 75-250B; ⏰11am-9pm; ❄ S Siam exit 2)

Sra Bua by Kiin Kiin
THAI $$$

19 MAP P98, D3

Helmed by a Thai and a Dane whose Copenhagen restaurant, Kiin Kiin, snagged a Michelin star, Sra Bua takes a correspondingly international approach to Thai

MBK Food Island (p103)

Siam Square's Silver Screens

Each Bangkok mall has its own cinema, but few can rival **Paragon Cineplex** (02 129 4635; www.paragoncineplex.com; 5th fl, Siam Paragon, 991/1 Rama I; S Siam exits 3 & 5). In addition to 16 screens, more than 3000 seats and Thailand's largest IMAX screen, the options here include the Blue Ribbon Screen, a cinema with a maximum of 72 seats, where you're plied with pillows, blankets, complimentary snacks and drinks, and of course, a 15-minute massage; and Enigma, where in addition to a sofa-like love seat designed for couples, you'll be served cocktails and food (as well as blankets and a massage).

If you're looking for something with less glitz and a bit more character, consider the old-school stand-alone theatres just across the street, such as **Scala** (Map p98, B3; 02 251 2861; Soi 1, Siam Sq; S Siam exit 2) and **Lido** (Map p98, C3; 02 252 6498; www.apexsiam-square.com; btwn Soi 2 & Soi 3, Siam Sq; S Siam exit 2).

For film showtimes at theatres across Bangkok, check in with moveedoo (www.moveedoo.com).

food. Putting local ingredients through the wringer of molecular gastronomy, the couple have created unconventional Thai dishes such as 'tom kha snow, mushrooms and picked lemon'. (02 162 9000; www.kempinski.com/en/bangkok/siam-hotel/dining; ground fl, Siam Kempinski Hotel, 991/9 off Rama I; mains 550-890B, set meals 1350-3100B; noon-3pm & 6-10.30pm; ❄️ 🖊️; S Siam exits 3 & 5)

Drinking

Hair of the Dog BAR

20 MAP P98, H4

The craft-beer craze that has swept Bangkok over the last few years is epitomised at this semi-concealed bar. With a morgue theme, dozens of bottles and 13 rotating taps, it's a great place for a weird, hoppy night. (www.hairofthedogbkk.com; 1st fl, Mahathun Plaza, 888/26 Th Phloen Chit; 5pm-midnight; S Phloen Chit exit 2)

Hyde & Seek BAR

21 MAP P98, H4

The tasty and comforting English-inspired bar snacks and meals here have earned Hyde & Seek the right to call itself a 'gastro bar'. But we reckon the real reasons to come are one of Bangkok's best-stocked liquor cabinets and some of the city's tastiest and most sophisticated cocktails. (www.hydeandseek.com; ground fl, Athenee Residence, 65/1 Soi Ruam Rudi; ⏱4.30pm-1am; §Phloen Chit exit 4)

Red Sky BAR

22 🚇 MAP P98, E3

Perched on the 55th floor of a sky-scraper smack-dab in the modern centre of Bangkok, Red Sky pro-vides one of Bangkok's most stun-ning rooftop views. The dramatic arch and all that glass provide the bar with a more upscale feel than Bangkok's other rooftoppers. (www.centarahotelsresorts.com; 55th fl, Centara Grand, CentralWorld, Th Ratchadamri; ⏱6pm-1am; §Chit Lom exit 9 to Sky Walk, Siam exit 6 to Sky Walk)

Co-Co Walk BAR

23 🚇 MAP P98, B2

This covered compound is a loud, messy smorgasbord of pubs, bars and live music popular with Thai university students on a night out. We'd list a few specific locales here, but they'd most likely all have changed names by the time you read this – it's just that kinda place. (87/70 Th Phayathai; ⏱5pm-midnight; §Ratchathewi exit 2)

Roof BAR

24 🚇 MAP P98, A3

In addition to views of central Bangkok from 25 floors up, the Roof offers a dedicated personal

martini sommelier and an exten-sive wine and champagne list. Party House One, on the ground floor of the same building, offers live music most nights. (www.siamatsiam.com/dining/roof; 25th fl, Siam@Siam, 865 Rama I; ⏱6pm-12.30am; §National Stadium exit 1)

Foreign Correspondents' Club of Thailand BAR

25 🚇 MAP P98, F4

A bar-restaurant, not to mention a bona fide gathering place for the city's hacks and photogs, the FCCT also hosts art exhibitions ranging in genre from photojour-nalism to contemporary painting (and there's live jazz on Friday nights). Check the website to see what's on when you're in town. (FCCT; www.fccthai.com; Penthouse, Maneeya Center, 518/5 Th Phloen Chit; ⏱noon-2.30pm & 6pm-mid-night Mon-Fri; §Chit Lom exit 2)

Making Sense of Street Names

Bangkok street names often seem unpronounceable; the inconsistency of romanised Thai spellings doesn't help. For example, the street Th Ratch-adamri is sometimes spelt 'Rajdamri'. And one of the most popular locations for foreign embassies is known both as Wireless Rd and Th Witthayu (wí·tá·yú is Thai for 'radio').

Unearthing Unique Souvenirs

Bangkok's malls are dominated by international brands, but there are some unique local outlets to consider.

The Selected (www.facebook.com/theselected; 3rd fl, Siam Center, Rama I; ⏱10am-9pm; S Siam exit 1) A carefully curated assemblage of modern, mostly Thai-made housewares, knick-knacks, clothing and accessories.

Karmakamet (www.karmakamet.co.th; 3rd fl, CentralWorld, Th Ratchadamri; ⏱10am-9.30pm; S Chit Lom exit 9 to Sky Walk, Siam exit 6 to Sky Walk) This brand's scented candles, incense, essential oils and other fragrant and nonfragrant items double both as classy housewares and unique souvenirs.

it's going green (ground fl, Bangkok Art & Culture Center, cnr Th Phayathai & Rama I; ⏱10.30am-8pm; S National Stadium exit 3) This boutique is also a good place to pick up retro Thai-style homewares, soaps and other items that double as one-of-a-kind souvenirs.

Objects of Desire Store (ODS; www.facebook.com/objectsofdesire store; 3rd fl, Siam Discovery, cnr Rama I & Th Phayathai; ⏱10am-10pm; S Siam exit 1) An open-air boutique specialising in design-focused contemporary ceramics, paper products, furniture and other homewares, most of which are made by Thai artisans.

Entertainment

Rock Pub

LIVE MUSIC

26 ⭐ MAP P98, B2

With posters of Iron Maiden as interior design and black jeans and long hair as the dress code, this long-standing, cave-like, live-music bar is Thailand's unofficial Embassy of Heavy Metal. (www.facebook.com/therockpub; 93/26-28 Th Phayathai; ⏱7pm-1am; S Ratchathewi exit 2)

Diplomat Bar

LIVE MUSIC

27 ⭐ MAP P98, G6

Named for its location in the middle of the embassy district, this is one of the few hotel lounges that locals make a point of visiting. Choose from an expansive list of innovative martinis, and sip to live jazz, played gracefully at conversation level. The live music starts at 8pm from Monday to Thursday, and at 8.30pm on Friday and Saturday. (ground fl, Conrad Hotel, 87 Th Witthayu/Wireless Rd; ⏱7pm-1am Mon-Thu, to 2am Fri & Sat; S Phloen Chit exit 5)

Shopping

Siam Discovery SHOPPING CENTRE

28 🔒 MAP P98, B3

With an open, almost-market-like feel and an impressive variety of unique goods ranging from housewares to clothing (including lots of items by Thai designers), the recently renovated Siam Discovery is hands down the most design-conscious mall in town. (www.siamdiscovery.co.th; cnr Rama I & Th Phayathai; ⊘10am-10pm; Ⓢ Siam exit 1)

MBK Center SHOPPING CENTRE

29 🔒 MAP P98, B3

This eight-storey market in a mall has emerged as one of Bangkok's top attractions. On any given weekend half of Bangkok's residents (and most of its tourists) can be found here combing through a seemingly inexhaustible range of small stalls, shops and merchandise. (www.mbk-center.com; cnr Rama I & Th Phayathai; ⊘10am-10pm; Ⓢ National Stadium exit 4)

Siam Square SHOPPING CENTRE

30 🔒 MAP P98, C4

This open-air shopping zone is ground zero for teenage culture in Bangkok. Pop music blares out of tinny speakers, and gangs of hipsters in various costumes ricochet between fast-food restaurants and closet-sized boutiques. It's a great place to pick up labels and designs

Siam Square

PUMIDOL/SHUTTERSTOCK ©

you're guaranteed not to find any-where else, though most outfits require a barely there waistline. (Rama I; ⏰11am-9pm; 🐾; Ⓢ Siam exits 2, 4 & 6)

Siam Center   SHOPPING CENTRE

31 🔒 MAP P98, C3

Siam Center, Thailand's first shopping centre, was built in 1976 but barely shows its age due to a recent nip and tuck. Its 3rd floor is one of the best locations to check out established local labels such as Food Republic (p106), **Flynow III** (www.flynowiii.com; 3rd fl, ⏰10am-9pm; Theatre and **Tango** (www.tangothailand.com; 3rd fl, ⏰10am-9pm). (www.siamcenter. co.th; Rama I; ⏰10am-9pm; Ⓢ Siam exit 1)

Platinum Fashion Mall   CLOTHING

32 🔒 MAP P98, E2

Linked with Bangkok's garment district, which lies just north across Th Phetchaburi, this five-storey mall is stocked with a seemingly never-ending selection of cheap, no-name couture. (www. platinumfashionmall.com; 644/3 Th Phetchaburi; ⏰9am-8pm; 🚤klorng boat to Pratunam Pier, Ⓢ Ratchathewi exit 4)

Siam Paragon   SHOPPING CENTRE

33 🔒 MAP P98, C3

As much air-conditioned urban park as it is a shopping centre, Siam Paragon is home to Sea Life Ocean World (p103), Paragon Cineplex (p108) and **Gourmet**

Siam Paragon

WITHGOD/SHUTTERSTOCK ©

Living Large

In your home town you may be considered average or even petite, but in Thailand you're likely an extra large, clearly marked on the tag as 'XL'. If that batters the body image, then skip the street markets, where the sizes are even smaller. Instead, for formal wear, many expats turn to custom tailors, while many of the vendors at Pratunam Market and several stalls on the 7th floor of MBK Center stock larger sizes.

Paradise (ground fl, Siam Paragon, 991/1 Rama I; mains 35-500B; ⊙10am-10pm; ❄ 🖉; Ṡ Siam exits 3 & 5), a huge basement-level food court. Then there are shops: on the 3rd floor is Kinokuniya, Thailand's largest English-language bookshop. (www.siamparagon.co.th; 991/1 Rama I; ⊙10am-10pm; Ṡ Siam exits 3 & 5)

CentralWorld   SHOPPING CENTRE

34 🔒 MAP P98, E3

Spanning eight storeys of more than 500 shops and 100 restaurants, CentralWorld is one of Southeast Asia's largest shopping centres. In addition to an ice rink, you'll find an extra-huge branch of bookshop B2S, and you could spend an hour sniffing around the fragrances at Karmakamet on the 3rd floor. (www.centralworld.co.th; Th Ratchadamri; ⊙10am-10pm; Ṡ Chit Lom exit 9 to Sky Walk, Siam exit 6 to Sky Walk)

Walking Tour 🚶

Victory Monument & Around

For a glimpse of Bangkok without the touts, tourists or malls (well, OK, some malls – this is, after all, Bangkok), take the BTS north to the area around the Victory Monument, where you'll find ordinary Thais doing ordinary Thai things, not to mention a handful of worthwhile attractions, good restaurants and fun bars.

Walk Facts

Start Suan Pakkad Palace Museum; **S** Phaya Thai exit 4

End Wine Pub; **S** Victory Monument exit 2

Length 3.8km; two to three hours

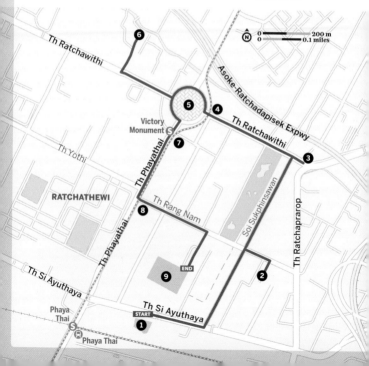

❶ Suan Pakkad Palace Museum

This **former royal residence** (วัง สวนผักกาด; Th Si Ayutthaya; 100B; ⏱9am-4pm) consists of eight traditional wooden Thai houses. Within the stilt buildings are displays of art, antiques and furnishings. The landscaped grounds are a peaceful oasis in an otherwise urban area.

❷ Raintree

Raintree (Soi Ruam Chit; ⏱6pm-1am Mon-Sat) is one of the few remaining places in town to host performances of 'songs for life', Thai folk music with roots in the communist insurgency of the 1960s and '70s. There are also tasty bar snacks.

❸ Pathé

The modern Thai equivalent of a 1950s-era American diner, **Pathé** (www.patherestaurant.com; 507 Th Ratchawithi; mains 95-275B; ⏱10am-midnight) combines solid Thai food, a fun atmosphere and a jukebox playing scratched records.

❹ Fashion Mall

Cheap underwear, domestic cosmetics, fake eyelashes and an entire zone of hair extensions – **Fashion Mall** (⏱10.30am-midnight) is the place to go to outfit yourself like a Thai university student on a budget.

❺ Victory Monument

The obelisk **Victory Monument** (อนุสาวรีย์ชัย; cnr Th Ratchawithi & Th Phayathai; ⏱24hr) was built by the then military government in 1941 to commemorate a 1940 campaign against the French in Laos.

❻ Toy

The surrounding the Victory Monument is home to heaps of simple restaurants selling spicy, rich 'boat noodles' – so-called because they used to be sold directly from boats that plied central Thailand's rivers and canals. Our pick of the lot is **Toy** (Soi 18, Th Ratchawithi, no Roman-script sign; mains from 15B; ⏱8am-5pm).

❼ Saxophone Pub & Restaurant

After more than 30 years, **Saxophone** (www.saxophonepub.com; 3/8 Th Phayathai; ⏱7.30pm-1.30am) remains one of Bangkok's premier live-music venues – a dark, intimate space where you sit just a few metres away from the band.

❽ Sky Train Jazz Club

This **club** (⏱5pm-2am) is more like the rooftop of your stoner buddy's flat than any jazz club we've ever been to. But that's what makes it so fun. To find it, look for the sign and proceed up the graffiti-covered stairway until you reach the roof.

❾ Wine Pub

If the upmarket but chilled setting and the DJ aren't reason enough to visit **Wine Pub** (www.winepubbang kok.com; 1st fl, Pullman Bangkok King Power, 8/2 Th Rang Nam; ⏱6.30pm-2am), the fact that it's one of the cheapest places in Bangkok to drink wine and nibble imported cheeses and cold cuts should be.

Explore

Riverside, Silom & Lumphini

Mae Nam Chao Phraya forms a watery backdrop to these linked neighbourhoods. History is still palpable in the riverside area's crumbling architecture, while heading inland, Silom is frenetic and modern, with lower Th Silom functioning as Bangkok's gaybourhood. Th Sathon is the much more subdued embassy zone and Lumphini is dominated by central Bangkok's largest green zone.

Get an early start at Lumphini Park (p122). Lunch on the famous fried chicken at Kai Thort Jay Kee (p126), then pop into Sri Mariamman Temple (p124). Spend the afternoon window shopping at House of Chao (p135). For dinner, consider a dinner cruise along the river. Alternatively, head inland for rooftop cocktails at Moon Bar (p130) followed by dinner at nahm (p125).

Getting There & Around

The Riverside area is ideal for an aimless wander among old buildings, and the BTS stop at Saphan Taksin is a good starting point. The BTS stop at Sala Daeng and the MRT stop at Si Lom put you at lower Th Silom, perfect jumping-off points for either Lumphini Park or the area's restaurants and sights.

S BTS To Riverside: Saphan Taksin. To Silom: Sala Daeng (interchange with MRT Si Lom). To Lumphini: Ratchadamri, Sala Daeng, Chong Nonsi and Surasak.

M To Silom: Si Lom (interchange with BTS Sala Daeng). To Lumphini: Lumphini.

Chao Phraya Express Boat To Riverside: River City Pier, Si Phraya Pier, Oriental Pier and Sathon/Central Pier. To Lumphini: Sathon/Central Pier.

Neighbourhood Map on p120

Lumphini Park (p122) PATCHRA SUTTIVIRAT/SHUTTERSTOCK ©

Walking Tour 🚶

Gay Silom

The side streets off lower Th Silom are so camp that they make San Francisco look like rural Texas. In addition to heaps of gay locals and tourists, the area is also home to a smattering of massage parlours and saunas, the in-your-face sex shows of nearby Duangthawee Plaza, the chilled open-air bars on Soi 4 and the clubs near Soi 2.

Walk Facts

Start Telephone Pub; Ⓜ Si Lom exit 2, Ⓢ Sala Daeng exit 1

End DJ Station; Ⓜ Si Lom exit 2, Ⓢ Sala Daeng exit 1

Length 1km; three to six hours

❶ Telephone & Balcony

Commence your evening on Soi 4, arguably Bangkok's pinkest street. It's packed with predominantly gay shops, bars, clubs and restaurants. The best views of the action are from long-standing street-side bars **Telephone Pub** (www.telephonepub.com; 114/11-13 Soi 4, Th Silom; ◷6pm-1am; 🛜) and, directly across the street, **Balcony** (www.balconypub.com; 86-88 Soi 4, Th Silom; ◷5.30pm-2am; 🛜).

❷ The Stranger

The Stranger (www.facebook.com/thestrangerbar; Soi 4, Th Silom; ◷5.45pm-2am) is probably the most low-key, sophisticated venue on Soi 4 – except during the drag shows on Monday, Friday and Saturday nights.

❸ Banana Club on 4

An inviting open-air balcony, sultry, curtained private lounges, and an intimate club, **Banana Bar** (114/17-18 Soi 4, Th Silom; ◷7pm-2am) is the one-stop-shop for a fabulously gay night out.

❹ Duangthawee Plaza

Finding the Soi 4 scene a tad too tame? Cross over to **Duangthawee Plaza** (Soi Twilight; Soi Pratuchai; ◷7pm-1am), a strip of male-only go-go bars (sample names: Hot Male, Banana Bar, Dream Boy) that is the gay equivalent of nearby Th Patpong. Expect tacky sex shows performed by bored-looking young men.

❺ White Rabbit

Take a breather, fuel up, or simply partake in one of the area's more low-key gay scenes at this **cafe/restaurant/lounge bar** (12/3 Th Silom; ◷11am-1am; 🛜).

❻ DJ Station

DJ Station (www.dj-station.com; 8/6-8 Soi 2, Th Silom; admission from 150B; ◷10pm-2am) is one of Bangkok's most legendary gay dance clubs. Get there at 11.30pm for the nightly cabaret show, or later for a packed house of Thai guppies (gay professionals), prostitutes and a few Westerners. There are several similar dance clubs and bars crammed into this tiny street. Admission ranges from 150B to 300B.

A **B** **C** **D**

Riverside, Silom & Lumphini

1

Th Charoen Krung

Rama IV

TALAT NOI

Th Maha Phrutharam

Phayathai–Bangkok Expwy
Th Maha Nakhon

Rama IV

Sam Yan Ⓜ

2

Marine Department Pier

River City Pier 🄰43

17

Si Phraya Pier

Th Si Phraya

BANGRAK

Th Naret

Th Sap

Th Surawong

Soi 39

42 🄰

Soi 43

Bangkokian Museum 2

Neilson Hays Library 9

Th Surawong

Soi 21

21

16

Th Decho

41 🄰

3

Thailand-Creative & Design Center

Soi 32

11

Old Customs House

10

39

24 ✕

🄰47

Soi 40 (Soi Oriental)

Oriental Pier

Th Mahesak

Th Surawong

Soi 20

Soi 26

Soi 30

Sri Mariamman Temple

8

Th Silom

Kathmandu Photo Gallery

23 ✕

29

Health Land 3

4

14 ✕

Mae Nam Chao Phraya

46 🄰

32

Soi 44

Soi 46

30

Number 1 Gallery

Th Pramuan

Soi 19

19

Th Pan

18

Soi 12

Soi 10

Th Si Wiang

Th Surasak

Soi 21

Saphan Taksin

Saphan Taksin

Th Sathon Neua (North)

Th Sathon Tai (South)

Surasak Ⓢ

Soi St Louis 2

Soi St Louis 3

5

Sathon/ Central Pier

Soi 51

Sathorn Unique Tower 4

Phayathai–Bangkok Expwy

Soi St Louis 2

Th Charoen Krung

6

37

🄰40

Ⓝ

0 —————— 500 m
0 —————— 0.25 miles

For reviews see	
⊙ Sights	p122
✕ Eating	p125
🄿 Drinking	p130
✪ Entertainment	p133
🄰 Shopping	p135

E

F
Royal
Bangkok
Sports Club

G

H

1

Chulalongkorn
University

Th Langsuan

Th Henri Dunant

Th Sarasin

Queen
Saovabha
Memorial
Institute ⊙7

Soi Sanam
Khli (Polo)
⊗15

Rama IV

SILOM

Soi
Phat Pong 2

Th Ratchadamri

Lumphini
Park

Th Witthayu (Wireless Rd)

2

Th
Phat Pong

1

44

45 ⊕49
48 ⊕ Soi 4
⊕ Sala Daeng

M Si Lom

Rama IV

36
⊕
Th Silom

22 ⊕
28 ⊕

Soi 3

Th Convert

Soi Sala
Daeng 2

Th Sala Daeng

Soi Sala Daeng 1

38

31

M Lumphini

3

27

Th Sathon Tai (South)

Chong
Nonsi
⑤

Soi Phiphat 2

13

Ruen-Nuad
Massage Studio

5

⊗12

26

Bangkok
CityCity
Gallery

34
⊕

Th Sathon Neua (North)
Th Sathon Tai (South)

Soi 3

Soi Nantha-Mozart

Soi 1

33
⊘4

Soi Si
Bamphen

Soi 7
⊙ MR Kukrit
6 Pramoj House

25 ⊕

Th Naradhiwas Rajanagarindra (Chong Nonsi)

Soi Suan Phlu

Soi Ngam Du Phli

Soi Suanphlu 1

SATHON

Soi Ngam Duphli

5
⊗
20

Th Yen Akat

6

⊕35

E

F

G

H

Sights

Lumphini Park PARK

1 ◎ MAP P120, G2

Named after the Buddha's place of birth in Nepal, Lumphini Park is the best way to escape Bangkok without actually leaving town. Shady paths, a large artificial lake and swept lawns temporarily blot out the roaring traffic and hulking concrete towers. (สวนลุมพินี; bounded by Th Sarasin, Rama IV, Th Witthayu/Wireless Rd & Th Ratchadamri; ◷4.30am-9pm; 👪; MLumphini exit 3, Si Lom exit 1, ⓈSala Daeng exit 3, Ratchadamri exit 2)

Bangkokian Museum MUSEUM

2 ◎ MAP P120, B3

A collection of three antique structures built during the early 20th century, the Bangkokian Museum illustrates an often-overlooked period of the city's history and functions as a peek into a Bangkok that, these days, is disappearing at a rapid pace. (พิพิธภัณฑ์ชาวบางกอก; 273 Soi 43, Th Charoen Krung; admission by donation; ◷10am-4pm Wed-Sun; 🚢Si Phraya/River City Pier)

Health Land MASSAGE

3 ◎ MAP P120, D4

This, the main branch of a long-standing Thai massage mini-empire, offers good-value, no-nonsense massage and spa treatments in a tidy environment. (☎02 637 8883; www.healthlandspa.

com; 120 Th Sathon Neua/North; 2hr massage 550B; ◷9am-11pm; ⓈSurasak exit 3)

Sathorn Unique Tower NOTABLE BUILDING

4 ◎ MAP P120, B5

In 1990 construction began on Sathorn Unique, known colloquially as the Ghost Tower because locals believe the plot of land it occupies to be a former cemetery. In 1997, with an estimated 75% of the tower completed, the Asian crisis reached its peak, funds disappeared and construction was simply halted, leaving it in its partially finished state ever since. (Soi 51, Th Charoen Krung; 🚢Sathon/Central Pier, ⓈSaphan Taksin)

Ruen-Nuad Massage Studio MASSAGE

5 ◎ MAP P120, F3

Set in a refurbished wooden house, this charming place successfully avoids both the tackiness and New Agedness that characterise most Bangkok Thai-massage joints. Prices are relatable, too. (☎02 632 2662; 42 Th Convent; massage per hour 350B; ◷10am-9pm; MSi Lom exit 2, ⓈSala Daeng exit 2)

MR Kukrit Pramoj House HISTORIC BUILDING

6 ◎ MAP P120, E4

Author and statesman Mom Ratchawong Kukrit Pramoj (1911–95) once resided in this charming complex now open to the public. Surrounded by a manicured garden, the five teak buildings introduce visitors to traditional Thai architecture, arts and the former resident, who served as prime minister of Thailand in 1974 and '75, wrote more than 150 books and spent 20 years decorating the house. (บ้านหม่อมราชวงศ์คึกฤทธิ์ ปราโมช; 📞 02 286 8185; Soi 7, Th Naradhiwas Rajanagarindra/Chong Nonsi; adult/child 50/20B; 🕙10am-4pm; S Chong Nonsi exit 2)

Queen Saovabha Memorial Institute
ZOO

7 ◉ MAP P120, E2

Thailand's snake farms tend to gravitate towards carnivalesque rather than humanitarian, except at the Queen Saovabha Memorial Institute. Founded in 1923, the snake farm gathers antivenom by milking the snakes' venom, injecting it into horses, and harvesting and purifying the antivenom they produce. The antivenoms are then used to treat human victims of snake bites. Regular milkings (11am Monday to Friday) and snake-handling performances (2.30pm Monday to Friday and 11am Saturday and Sunday) are held at the outdoor amphitheatre. (สถานเสาวภา, Snake Farm; cnr Rama IV & Th Henri Dunant; adult/child 200/50B; 🕙9.30am-3.30pm Mon-Fri, to 1pm Sat & Sun; 👫; M Si Lom exit 1, S Sala Daeng exit 3)

Sri Mariamman Temple (p124)

Silom's Art Galleries

Upper Th Silom and around is home to some of Bangkok's better art galleries:

Kathmandu Photo Gallery (Map p120, C4; www.kathmanduphotobkk. com; 87 Th Pan; admission free; ⏰11am-7pm Tue-Sun; Ⓢ Surasak exit 3) Bangkok's only gallery wholly dedicated to photography.

Bangkok CityCity Gallery (Map p121, H4; ☎ 083 087 2725; www.bang-kokcitycity.com; 13/3 Soi 1, Th Sathon Tai/South; admission free; ⏰1-7pm Wed-Sun; Ⓜ Lumphini exit 2) Small, modern-feeling gallery hosting the work of domestic, often pop-inspired artists, and the occasional performance.

Number 1 Gallery (Map p120, B4; www.number1gallery.com; 19 Soi 21, Th Silom; admission free; ⏰10am-7pm Mon-Sat; Ⓢ Surasak exit 3) Relatively new gallery featuring the often attention-grabbing work of Thai artists.

Gallery VER (☎ 02 103 4067; www.vergallery.com; 10 Soi 22, Th Narathiwat Ratchanakharin/Chong Nonsi; admission free; ⏰noon-6pm Tue-Sun; Ⓢ Chong Nonsi exit 2 & taxi) A vast art space with work by both established and emerging domestic artists, sometimes with a subversive lean.

Sri Mariamman Temple

HINDU TEMPLE

8 ◉ MAP P120, C3

Arrestingly flamboyant, the Sri Mariamman Hindu temple is a wild collision of colours, shapes and deities. It was built in the 1860s by Tamil immigrants and features a 6m facade of intertwined, full-colour Hindu deities. While most of the people working in the temple hail from the Indian subcontinent, you will likely see plenty of Thai and Chinese devotees praying here as well. This is because the Hindu gods figure just as prominently in their individualistic approach to religion. (วัดพระศรีมหาอุมาเทวี/วัด

แขก, Wat Phra Si Maha Umathewi; cnr Th Silom & Th Pan; admission free; ⏰6am-8pm Mon-Thu, to 9pm Fri, to 8.30pm Sat & Sun; Ⓢ Surasak exit 3)

Neilson Hays Library

LIBRARY

9 ◉ MAP P120, C3

The oldest English-language library in Thailand, the Neilson Hays dates back to 1922 and today remains the city's noblest place for a read – with the added benefit of air-con. It has a good selection of children's books and a decent range of titles on Thailand. (www.neilsonhayslibrary. com; 195 Th Surawong; non-members 50B; ⏰9.30am-5pm Tue-Sun; Ⓢ Surasak exit 3)

Old Customs House
HISTORIC BUILDING

10 ◎ MAP P120, A3

The country's former Customs House was once the gateway to Thailand, levying taxes on traders moving in and out of the kingdom. It was designed by an Italian architect and built in the 1890s; the front door opened onto its source of income (the river) and the grand facade was ceremoniously decorated in columns and transom windows. (กรมศุลกากร; Soi 36, Th Charoen Krung; 🚢 Oriental Pier)

Thailand Creative & Design Center
LIBRARY

11 ◎ MAP P120, B3

Taking up a sizeable chunk of Bangkok's art deco main post office is this new 'playground for creativity'. In practical terms, that means an art- and design-heavy research library, work spaces, gallery space and a cafe, all in a package that screams to be Instagrammed. Non-members can purchase a day pass to the facilities for 100B. (TCDC, ศูนย์สร้างสรรค์ งานออกแบบ; 🕿 02 105 7400; www. tcdc.or.th; 1160 Th Charoen Krung; 🕑 10.30am-9pm Tue-Sun)

Eating

nahm
THAI $$$

12 🍴 MAP P120, G3

Australian chef-author David Thompson is the man behind one of Bangkok's – and if you believe the critics, the world's – best Thai restaurants. Using ancient cookbooks as his inspiration, Thompson has given new life to previously extinct dishes with exotic descriptions such as 'smoked fish curry with prawns, chicken livers, cockles, chillies and black pepper'. (🕿 02 625 3388; www. comohotels.com; ground fl, Metropolitan Hotel, 27 Th Sathon Tai/South; set lunch 600-1600B, set dinner 2500B, mains 310-800B; 🕑 noon-2pm Mon-Fri, 7-10.30pm daily; ❄; Ⓜ Lumphini exit 2)

Eat Me
INTERNATIONAL $$$

13 🍴 MAP P120, E3

With descriptions like 'charred witlof and mozzarella salad with preserved lemon and dry-aged Cecina beef', the dishes may sound all over the map or perhaps somewhat pretentious, but they're actually just plain tasty. A casual yet sophisticated atmosphere, excellent cocktails,

Making Reservations

If you have a lot of friends in tow or will be attending a formal restaurant (including hotel restaurants), reservations are recommended. Bookings are also recommended for Sunday brunches and dinner cruises. Otherwise, you generally won't have a problem scoring a table at the vast majority of restaurants in Bangkok.

The End of Street Food?

In mid-2017, media outlets reported that food stalls and vendors were slated to be banned from the streets of Bangkok.

Locals and visitors were shocked and appalled. The Tourism Authority of Thailand (TAT) rushed into repair mode. Even Thailand's Ministry of Foreign Affairs felt obligated to release a statement. Within days the Bangkok Metropolitan Authority (BMA), the organisation which released the statement and the entity responsible for overseeing street vendors, back-pedalled, claiming that it was misquoted and that it was simply planning to enforce already existing laws and regulations.

What does this mean for Bangkok's estimated 20,000 street vendors? As with many things in Thailand, the answer is unclear. At press time, the BMA had deployed a team of officers to enforce rules and regulations in Banglamphu and Chinatown, but remained vague about its plans to deal with street food in other parts of the city. For now, the situation appears to be at a stalemate, but other factors, including private development, have already done away with some of Bangkok's most famous curbside eats. It seems likely that in the future the city's streets may be cleaner and clearer, if a lot less delicious.

a handsome wine list and some of the city's best desserts also make this one of our favourite places in Bangkok to dine. (📞02 238 0931; www.eatmerestaurant.com; Soi Phiphat 2; mains 300-1400B; ⏰3pm-1am; ❄️🍸; Ⓜ️Si Lom exit 2, Ⓢ Sala Daeng exit 2)

Muslim Restaurant   THAI $

14 🍴 MAP P120, B4

Plant yourself in any random wooden booth of this ancient eatery for a glimpse into what restaurants in Bangkok used to be like. The menu, much like the interior design, doesn't appear to have

changed much in the restaurant's 70-year history, and the biryanis, curries and samosas remain more Indian-influenced than Thai. (1354-6 Th Charoen Krung; mains 40-140B; ⏰6.30am-5.30pm; 🚢Oriental Pier, Ⓢ Saphan Taksin exit 1)

Kai Thort Jay Kee   THAI $$

15 🍴 MAP P120, H2

Although the sôm·đam (spicy green papaya salad), sticky rice and lâhp (a spicy salad of minced meat) of this former street stall give the impression of a north-eastern-Thai-style eatery, the restaurant's namesake deep-fried bird is more southern in origin. Regardless, smothered in a thick layer of crispy deep-fried garlic, it is nothing but a truly Bangkok experience. (Polo Fried Chicken; 137/1-3 Soi Sanam Khli/Polo; mains 50-350B; ⊘11am-9pm; ❄; Ⓜ Lumphini exit 3)

Soi 10 Food Centres   THAI $

16 ⊗ MAP P120, D3

These two adjacent hangar-like buildings tucked behind Soi 10 are the main lunchtime fuelling stations for the area's office staff. Choices range from southern-style *kôw gaang* (point-and-choose curries ladled over rice) to just about every incarnation of Thai noodle. (Soi 10, Th Silom; mains 20-60B; ⊘8am-3pm Mon-Fri; Ⓜ Si Lom exit 2, ⓢ Sala Daeng exit 1)

Never Ending Summer   THAI $$$

17 ⊗ MAP P120, A2

The cheesy name doesn't do justice to this surprisingly sophisticated Thai restaurant located in a former warehouse by the river. Join Bangkok's beautiful crowd for antiquated Thai dishes such as cubes of watermelon served with a dry 'dressing' of fish, sugar and deep-fried shallots, or fragrant green curry with pork and fresh bird's-eye chilli. (📞02 861 0953; www.facebook.com/theneverending summer; 41/5 Th Charoen Nakhon; mains 200-1000B; ⊘11am-11pm; ❄; 🚤river-crossing ferry from River City Pier)

Street food stall, Silom

Dinner Cruises

Several companies run dinner cruises along Mae Nam Chao Phraya. Tickets range from 1500B to 1700B. Cruises last two hours and depart from River City Pier. Your one-stop centre for all your cruise needs is the **River City Information Desk** (www.rivercity.co.th; ground fl, River City, 23 Th Yotha; ⊙10am-10pm; ⛴Si Phraya/River City Pier, or shuttle boat from Sathon/Central Pier), from which tickets can be purchased for:

Grand Pearl (✆ 02 861 0255; www.grandpearlcruise.com; cruises 2000B; ⊙ cruise 7.30-9.30pm)

Chaophraya Cruise (✆ 02 541 5599; www.chaophrayacruise.com; cruises 1700B; ⊙ cruise 7-9pm)

Wan Fah (✆ 02 622 7657; www.wanfah.in.th; cruises 1500B; ⊙ cruise 7-9pm)

Chao Phraya Princess (✆ 02 860 3700; www.thaicruise.com; cruises 1500B; ⊙ cruise 7-9.30pm)

White Orchid (✆ 02 438 8228; www.whiteorchidrivercruise.com; cruises 1400B; ⊙ cruise 7.20-9.45pm)

Supanniga Cruise (✆ 02 714 7608; www.supannigacruise.com; cruises 1250-3250B; ⊙ cruises 4.45-5.45pm & 6.15-8.30pm)

Chennai Kitchen INDIAN $

 18   MAP P120, C4

This thimble-sized mum-and-dad restaurant puts out some of the best southern Indian vegetarian food in town. The metre-long *dosai* (a crispy southern Indian bread) is always a good choice, but if you're feeling indecisive (or exceptionally famished) go for the banana-leaf thali (set meal) that seems to incorporate just about everything in the kitchen. (107/4 Th Pan; mains 70-150B; ⊙10am-3pm & 6-9.30pm; ❄🍸; Ⓢ Surasak exit 3)

Taling Pling THAI $$

19   MAP P120, C4

Don't be fooled by the flashy interior; long-standing Taling Pling continues to serve a thick menu of homey, full-flavoured Thai dishes. It's a good starting point for rich, southern and central Thai fare such as *gaang kôo·a* (crabmeat curry with wild betel leaves), with tasty pies and cakes and refreshing drinks rounding out the choices. (Baan Silom, Soi 19, Th Silom; mains 110-275B; ⊙11am-10pm; ❄🍸; Ⓢ Surasak exit 3)

Issaya Siamese Club

THAI $$$

20 MAP P120, H5

Housed in a charming 1920s-era villa, Issaya is Thai celebrity-chef Ian Kittichai's first effort at a domestic outpost serving the food of his homeland. Dishes alternate between somewhat saucy, meaty items and lighter dishes using produce from the restaurant's organic garden.The restaurant can be a bit tricky to find, and is best approached in a taxi via Soi Ngam Du Phli. (☏02 672 9040; www.issaya.com; 4 Soi Sri Aksorn; mains 150-600B; ☉11.30am-2.30pm & 6-10.30pm; ❄🌿; Ⓜ Khlong Toei exit 1 & taxi)

Somboon Seafood

CHINESE $$$

21 MAP P120, D3

Somboon, a hectic seafood hall with a reputation far and wide, is known for doing the best curry-powder crab in town. Soy-steamed sea bass (plah grà·pong nêung see·éw) is also a speciality and, like all good Thai seafood, should be enjoyed with an immense platter of kôw pàt boo (fried rice with crab) and as many friends as you can gather together. (☏02 233 3104; www.somboonseafood.com; cnr Th Surawong & Th Naradhiwas Rajanagarindra/Chong Nonsi; mains 120-900B; ☉4-11pm; ❄; Ⓢ Chong Nonsi exit 3)

Somtam Convent

THAI $

22 MAP P120, E3

Northeastern-style Thai food is usually relegated to less-than-hygienic stalls perched by the side of the road with no menu or English-speaking staff in sight. A less intimidating introduction to the wonders of lâhp (a minced-meat 'salad'), sôm·đam (papaya salad) and other Isan (northeastern Thai) delights can be had at this popular and long-standing restaurant. ('Hai'; 2/4-5 Th Convent; mains 60-160B; ☉11am-9pm Mon-Fri, to 5pm Sat; ❄; Ⓜ Si Lom exit 2, Ⓢ Sala Daeng exit 2)

Bunker

AMERICAN $$$

23 MAP P120, D4

Bunker's menu, vibe, ace cocktail menu and swish service make you feel like you're in Manhattan, except that here in Bangkok, the dining room is spacious, not elbow-to-elbow. Tapas, sharing plates and hearty mains range from plant-based (endive and sunchoke salad) to high-quality meats (wagyu short ribs), and make this a good spot for a special occasion. (☏02 234 7749; www.bunkerbkk.com; 118/2 Soi 12, Th Sathon Nuea; mains 450-900B; ☉5.30-11pm; Ⓢ Chong Nonsi exit 3)

Le Normandie

FRENCH $$$

24 MAP P120, A4

Although today's Bangkok boasts a plethora of upmarket choices, Le Normandie has maintained its niche and is still the only place to go for a genuinely old-world 'Continental' dining experience. A revolving cast of Michelin-starred guest chefs and some of the world's most decadent ingredients keep up the standard, and appropriately formal attire (including jacket) is required. Book ahead. (📞02 659 9000; www. mandarinoriental.com; Mandarin Oriental, 48 Soi 40/Oriental, Th Charoen Krung; mains 2100-3300B; ⏱noon-2.30pm & 7-11pm Mon-Sat, 7-11pm Sun; ❄; ⛴Oriental Pier or hotel shuttle boat from Sathon/Central Pier)

Drinking

Smalls   BAR

25 🚇 MAP P120, F4

Even though it only opened its doors in 2014, Smalls is the kind of bar that feels like it's been here forever. Fixtures include a cheekily decadent interior, an inviting rooftop, food-themed nights (check the Facebook page) and live jazz on Wednesdays. The eclectic house cocktails are strong, if sweet, and bar snacks range from rillettes to quesadillas. (www.face book.com/smallsbkk; 186/3 Soi Suan Phlu; ⏱8.30pm-late; 🚇Lumphini exit 2 & taxi)

Moon Bar   BAR

26 🚇 MAP P120, G3

An alarmingly short barrier at this rooftop bar is all that separates patrons from the street, 61 floors down. Located on top of the Banyan Tree Hotel, Moon Bar claims to be among the highest alfresco bars in the world. It's also a great place from which to see the Phrapradaeng Peninsula, a vast green area that's colloquially known as Bangkok's green lung. (www.banyantree.

com; 61st fl, Banyan Tree Hotel, 21/100 Th Sathon Tai/South; ⏱5pm-1am; 🚇Lumphini exit 2)

Ceresia   CAFE

27 🚇 MAP P120, F3

Finally, a local roastery to rescue us from the caffeinated shackles of you-know-who. And best of all, boasting high-quality exotic and domestic beans, expertly prepared drinks and good pastries, Ceresia is more than just an alternative. (ground fl, Tisco Tower, 48/2 Th Sathon Neua/North; ⏱8am-6pm Mon-Fri, 9am-6pm Sat; 🚇Lumphini exit 2)

Vesper   BAR

28 🚇 MAP P120, E3

One of the freshest faces on Bangkok's drinking scene is this deceptively classic-feeling bar-restaurant. As the name suggests, the emphasis here is on cocktails, including several revived classics and mixed drinks mellowed by ageing for six weeks in white-oak barrels. (www.vesperbar.co; 10/15 Th Convent; ⏱noon-2.30pm & 6pm-1am Mon-Fri, 6pm-midnight Sat, noon-2.30pm Sun; Ⓜ Si Lom exit 2, Ⓢ Sala Daeng exit 2)

Namsaah Bottling Trust   BAR

29 🚇 MAP P120, D3

Namsaah is all about twists. From its home (a former mansion incongruously painted hot pink) to the cocktails (classics with a tweak or two) and the bar snacks and dishes (think *pàt tai* with foie gras), everything's a little bit off in just the right way. (www.namsaah.com; 401 Soi 7, Th Silom; ☺5pm-2am; Ⓜ Si Lom exit 2, Ⓢ Sala Daeng exit 2)

Maggie Choo's
BAR

31 🚌 MAP P120, B4

A former bank vault with a Chinatown-opium-den vibe, secret passageways and lounging women in silk dresses. With all this going on, it's easy to forget that Maggie Choo's is actually a bar, although you'll be reminded by the creative and somewhat sweet cocktails, and a crowd that blends selfie-snapping locals and curious tourists. (www.facebook.com/maggiechoos; basement, Novotel Bangkok Fenix Silom, 320 Th Silom; ☺7.30pm-2am Sun-Thu, to 3am Fri & Sat; Ⓢ Surasak exit 1)

Park Society
BAR

31 🚌 MAP P120, H3

Gazing down at the green expanse of Lumphini Park, abruptly bordered by tall buildings on most sides, you can be excused for thinking that Bangkok almost, kinda, sorta feels like Manhattan. The drink prices at Park Society, 29 floors above the ground, will also remind you of New York City, although there are monthly promotions. (29th fl, Sofitel So, 2 Th Sathon Neua/North; ☺5pm-2am; Ⓜ Lumphini exit 2)

Sky Bar
BAR

32 🚌 MAP P120, B4

Descend the Hollywood-like staircase to emerge at this bar that juts out over the city's skyline and Mae Nam Chao Phraya. This is the

Sky Bar

NIKADA/GETTY IMAGES ©

Patpong:
Tourists in the Go-Go Bar Zone

The neon signs leave little doubt about the dominant industry in Patpong, the world's most infamous strip of go-go bars and clubs running 'exotic' shows.

Roots in 'R&R'

Patpong occupies two soi that run between Th Silom and Th Surawong in Bangkok's financial district. The streets are privately owned by – and named for – the Chinese-Thai Patpongpanich family, who bought the land in the 1940s and built Patpong Soi 1 and its shophouses; Soi 2 was laid later. During the Vietnam War the first bars and clubs opened to cater to American soldiers on 'R&R'. The scene grew through the '70s and peaked in the '80s, when official Thai tourism campaigns made the sort of 'sights' available in Patpong a pillar of their marketing.

Prostitution in Thailand

Prostitution is illegal in Thailand but there are as many as two million sex workers, the vast majority of whom – women and men – cater to Thai men. Many come from poorer regional areas, such as Isan in the northeast, while others might be students helping themselves through university. Sociologists suggest Thais often view sex through a less moralistic filter than Westerners. That doesn't mean Thai wives like their husbands employing the services of sex workers, but it's only recently that the empowerment of women through education and employment has led to a more vigorous questioning of this very widespread practice.

Patpong Today

These days, Patpong has mellowed – somewhat. Thanks in part to the popular night market that fills the soi after 5pm, it draws so many tourists that it has become a sort of sex theme park. There are still plenty of the stereotypical middle-aged men ogling pole dancers, sitting in dark corners of the so-called 'blow-job bars' and paying 'bar fines' to take girls to hotels that charge by the hour. But you'll also be among other tourists and families who come to see what all the fuss is about.

classic Bangkok rooftop bar – scenes from *The Hangover Part II* were filmed here – and the views are breathtaking, although the excessive drink prices and selfie-snapping crowds have made it a hectic destination. (www.lebua.com; 63rd fl, State Tower, 1055 Th Silom;

⊙6pm-1am; 🚢Sathon/Central Pier; 🚊Saphan Taksin exit 3)

Wong's Place
BAR

33 🔍 MAP P120, H4

This dusty den is a time warp into the backpacker world of the early 1980s. The namesake owner died several years ago, but a relative removed the padlock and picked up where Wong left off. It works equally well as a destination or a last resort, but don't bother knocking until 1am, keeping in mind that it stays open until the last person crawls out. (27/3 Soi Si Bamphen; ⊙9pm-late Tue-Sun; 🚇Lumphini exit 1)

Cé La Vi
CLUB

34 🔍 MAP P120, E4

Spanning multiple bars, three restaurants and two clubs, Cé La Vi remains the biggest thing on Bangkok's club scene – literally and figuratively – although it must be said that there are more sophisticated places in town. Expect an entry fee of 300B after 10pm on Fridays and Saturdays. (www.bkk.celavi.com; 38th & 39th fl, Sathorn Sq Complex, 98 Th Sathon Neua/North; ⊙11am-1am Mon-Thu, to 3am Fri & Sat; 🚊Chong Nonsi exit 1)

Entertainment

Tawandang German Brewery
LIVE MUSIC

35 🔍 MAP P120, F6

It's Oktoberfest all year round at this hangar-sized music hall. The Thai-German food is tasty, the house-made brews are entirely potable, and the nightly stage shows make singing along a necessity. Music starts at 8.30pm. (www.tawandang.co.th; cnr Rama III & Th Narathiwat Ratchanakharin/Chong Nonsi; ⊙5pm-1am; 🚊Chong Nonsi exit 2 & taxi)

Bamboo Bar
LIVE MUSIC

After more than 60 years of service, the Mandarin Oriental's (see 24 🍽 Map p120, A4) Bamboo Bar remains one of the city's premier locales for live jazz. Guest vocalists are flown in from across the globe – check the website to see who's in town – and the music starts at 9pm nightly. (📞02 236 0400; ground fl; ⊙5pm-1am Sun-Thu, to 2am Fri & Sat; 🚢Oriental Pier or hotel shuttle boat from Sathon/Central Pier)

Whiteline
BAR

36 🔍 MAP P120, E3

This six-storey shophouse-turned-artspace in bustling Silom has something for everyone: film screenings, indie concerts, gallery nights displaying local talent and parties that rage late into the night. Drinks are simple Thai lagers and house spirits, with a few standout bottles of imported IPAs. Check the Facebook page for a current list of events. (📞087 061 1117; www.facebook.com/whitelinebangkok; Soi 8, Th Silom; ⊙7pm-midnight Thu-Sun; 🚇Si Lom exit 2, 🚊Sala Daeng exit 1)

Calypso Bangkok
CABARET

37 ⭐ MAP P120, A6

Located in Asiatique market, Calypso is yet another destination for *gà·teu·i* (also spelt *kàthoey*) cabaret, which features cross-dresser or transgender performers. (📞02 688 1415; www.calypsocabaret.com; Asiatique, Soi 72-76, Th Charoen Krung; adult/child 900/600B; ⏱show times 8.15pm & 9.45pm; ⛴shuttle ferry from Sathon/Central Pier)

Bangkok Screening Room
CINEMA

38 ⭐ MAP P120, G3

Bangkok has heaps of attractions that draw tourists in — great weather, fantastic bars, unbeatable food, low prices – but it's not known for being an arts haven.

This cinema is trying to change that, one indie film at a time. Check the website for the revolving list of films, but expect the roster to showcase the work of budding Thai filmmakers.

Book tickets a day in advance to score one of the 50 seats in the single-screen theatre and grab a craft beer before settling in. (www.bkksr.com; 8-9 Soi Sala Deang 1; Ⓜ Si Lom exit 2, Ⓢ Sala Daeng exit 4)

Sala Rim Naam
THEATRE

39 ⭐ MAP P120, A3

The historic Mandarin Oriental hosts dinner theatre in a sumptuous Thai pavilion located across the river in Thonburi. The price is well above the average, reflecting the means of the hotel's client base, but the performance

Asiatique

gets positive reviews. (☎02 437 3080; www.mandarinoriental.com/bangkok/fine-dining/sala-rim-naam; Mandarin Oriental hotel, Soi 40/Oriental, Th Charoen Krung; tickets adult/child 2000/1700B; ⏰dinner & show 8.15-9.30pm; 🚤Oriental Pier or hotel shuttle boat from Sathon/Central Pier)

Shopping

Asiatique   MARKET

40 🅰 MAP P120, A6

One of Bangkok's more popular night markets, Asiatique takes the form of warehouses of commerce next to Chao Phraya River. Expect clothing, handicrafts, souvenirs and quite a few dining and drinking venues.Frequent, free shuttle boats depart from Sathon/Central Pier from 4pm to 11.30pm. (Soi 72-76, Th Charoen Krung; ⏰4-11pm; 🚤shuttle boat from Sathon/Central Pier)

House of Chao   ANTIQUES

41 🅰 MAP P120, D3

This three-storey antique shop, appropriately located in an antique shophouse, has everything necessary to deck out your fantasy colonial-era mansion. Particularly interesting are the various weather-worn doors, doorways, gateways and trellises that can be found in the covered area behind the showroom. (9/1 Th Decho; ⏰9.30am-7pm; 🅂Chong Nonsi exit 3)

Warehouse 30   HOMEWARES

42 🅰 MAP P120, A3

The latest trend in Bangkok seems to be converting formerly utilitarian structures into hypercool destinations that blend artsy sophistication and commerce. Warehouse 30, the newest and most impressive of the lot, takes the form of a string of World War II–era go-downs housing a cafe, a high-end florist, and a shop selling curated vintage items, locally made homewares and a tiny organic grocery. (52-60 Soi 30, Th Charoen Krung; ⏰11am-8pm Mon-Fri, 10am-9pm Sat & Sun)

River City   ANTIQUES

43 🅰 MAP P120, A2

Several upscale art and antique shops occupy the 3rd and 4th floors of this riverside mall, but, as with many antique shops in Bangkok, the vast majority of pieces appear to come from Myanmar and, to a lesser extent, Cambodia.A free shuttle boat to River City departs from Sathon/Central Pier every 30 minutes, from 10am to 8pm. (www.rivercity.co.th; 23 Th Yotha; ⏰10am-10pm; 🚤Si Phraya/River City Pier, or shuttle boat from Sathon/Central Pier)

Jim Thompson   FASHION & ACCESSORIES

44 🅰 MAP P120, E2

This is the surviving business of the international promoter of Thai silk; the largest Jim Thompson shop sells colourful silk place mats, handkerchiefs, wraps and cushions. The styles and motifs appeal to older, somewhat more conservative tastes. (www.jimthompson.com; 9 Th Surawong; ⏱9am-9pm; Ⓜ Si Lom exit 2, Ⓢ Sala Daeng exit 3)

Tamnan Mingmuang

ARTS & CRAFTS

45 🔒 MAP P120, E3

As soon as you step through the doors of this museum-like shop, the earthy smell of dried grass and stained wood rushes to meet you. Rattan, *yahn lí·pow* (a fern-like vine) and water hyacinth woven into patterns, and coconut shells carved into delicate bowls, are among the exquisite pieces that will outlast flashier souvenirs available on the streets. (2nd fl, Thaniya Plaza, Th Thaniya; ⏱10am-7pm; Ⓜ Si Lom exit 2, Ⓢ Sala Daeng exit 1)

Chiang Heng

HOMEWARES

46 🔒 MAP P120, B4

In need of a handmade stainless-steel wok or a manually operated coconut-milk strainer? Then we suggest you stop by this third-generation family-run kitchen-supply shop. Even if your cabinets are already stocked, a visit here is a glance into the type of special-ised shops that are quickly disap-pearing from Bangkok. There's no English-language sign; look for the blue doors. (1466 Th Charoen Krung; ⏱10.30am-7pm; 🚢 Sathon/Central Pier, Ⓢ Saphan Taksin exit 3)

Patpong Night Market

Look out for Counterfeits

Bangkok is ground zero for the production and sale of counterfeit goods. Although the prices may be enticing, be sure to keep in mind that counterfeit goods are almost always as shoddy as they are cheap.

Thai Home Industries

ARTS & CRAFTS

47 🔒 MAP P120, B4

Much more fun than the typically faceless Bangkok handicraft shop, the selection at this temple-like structure includes attractive woven baskets, cotton farmer shirts, handsome stainless-steel flatware and delicate mother-of-pearl spoons. (35 Soi 40/Oriental, Th Charoen Krung; 🕑9am-6.30pm Mon-Sat; 🚤Oriental Pier)

Patpong Night Market

GIFTS & SOUVENIRS

48 🔒 MAP P120, E3

You'll be faced with the competing distractions of strip-clubbing and shopping in this infamous area. And true to the area's illicit leanings, pirated goods (in particular watches) make a prominent appearance even amid a wholesome crowd of families and strait-laced couples. Bargain with determination, as first-quoted prices tend to be astronomically high. (Th Phat Phong & Soi Phat Phong 2; 🕑6pm-midnight; Ⓜ Si Lom exit 2, Ⓢ Sala Daeng exit 1)

Everyday by Karmakamet

GIFTS & SOUVENIRS

49 🔒 MAP P120, F2

Part cafe, part showroom for the eponymous brand's vast selection of scented candles, incense, essential oils and other fragrant and nonfragrant items, Karmakamet is the ideal gift stop. (Soi Yada; 🕑10am-10pm; Ⓜ Si Lom exit 2, Ⓢ Sala Daeng exit 1)

Walking Tour 🥾

Riverside Architecture Ramble

Bangkok isn't generally known for its secular architecture, but the road that parallels Mae Nam Chao Phraya, Th Charoen Krung, is home to many of the city's noteworthy structures. The area was formerly the city's largest foreign enclave, and today continues to serve as a home to many of Bangkok's Muslim residents.

Walk Facts

Start Ⓢ Saphan Taksin

End Viva & Aviv; 🚤 Tha Si Phraya/River City

Length 3km; two to three hours

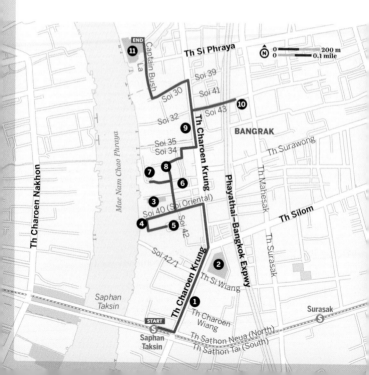

❶ Shophouses

Starting from the BTS at Saphan Taksin, walk north along Th Charoen Krung, passing the **ancient shophouses** between Th Charoen Wiang and Th Silom.

❷ State Tower

At the corner with Th Silom is the imposing and ugly neoclassical **State Tower**. If it's the afternoon, pop up to the 63rd floor for a drink at **Sky Bar** (Map p120, B4; www.lebua.com; 63rd fl, State Tower, 1055 Th Silom; ⏲6pm-1am).

❸ Mandarin Oriental

Turn left on Soi 40, home to the **Mandarin Oriental**, Bangkok's oldest and most storied hotel. The original 1887 structure remains today as the Author's Wing.

❹ East Asiatic Company

Across from the entrance of the Mandarin Oriental is the classical Venetian-style facade of the **East Asiatic Company**, built in 1901.

❺ Assumption Cathedral

Proceed beneath the overhead walkway linking two buildings to the red-brick **Assumption Cathedral**, which dates back to 1909.

❻ O.P. Place

Return to Soi 40 and take the first left. On your right is **O.P. Place**, today an antique mall, originally built in 1908 to house the German-owned Falck & Beidek Department Store.

❼ Old Customs House

Pass the French Embassy walls and turn left. Head towards the river and the 1890s-era **Old Customs House**.

❽ Haroon Village

Backtrack and turn left beneath the green sign that says 'Haroon Mosque'. You're now in **Haroon Village**, a Muslim enclave.

❾ General Post Office

Wind through Haroon and you'll eventually come to Soi 34, which leads back to Th Charoen Krung. Turn left and cross the street opposite the recently renovated art deco-style **General Post Office**.

❿ Bangkokian Museum

Head east on Soi 43 until you reach the **Bangkokian Museum** (พิพิธภัณฑ์ ชาวบางกอก; Map p120, B3; 273 Soi 43, Th Charoen Krung; admission by donation; ⏲10am-4pm Wed-Sun), a compound of three antique wooden homes.

⓫ Viva & Aviv

Cross Th Charoen Krung, enter Soi 30, and continue along Captain Bush Lane to River City – its riverside bar, **Viva & Aviv** (www.vivaaviv.com; ground fl, River City, 23 Th Yotha; ⏲11am-midnight), is a good place to end the walk.

Explore ✦

Thanon Sukhumvit

The BTS (Skytrain) stops are convenient ways to define Th Sukhumvit's various vibes. Lower Sukhumvit, particularly the area around Nana BTS station, is a discombobulating mix of sexpats and tourists. Middle Sukhumvit, around BTS Asok/MRT Sukhumvit, is dominated by midrange hotels, international restaurants and businesses. Near BTS Phrom Phong is where you'll find the well-concealed compounds of wealthy Thai residents and tidy Japanese enclaves. While extending east from BTS Ekkamai, the area feels more provincial and more Thai.

Begin your day with a swing through Khlong Toey Market (p144), central Bangkok's largest and most hectic market. Afterwards, ride the MRT to Siam Society & Kamthieng House (p144). Take advantage of Sukhumvit's spread of international cuisines with a Middle Eastern lunch at Nasir Al-Masri (p149). Kick the evening off with cocktails and art at WTF (p150). For dinner, consider upscale Thai at Bo.lan (p148). Continue with live music at The Living Room (p155).

Getting There & Around

The BTS runs along the length of Th Sukhumvit, making it a snap to reach just about anywhere around here.

S BTS Nana, Asok (interchange with MRT Sukhumvit), Phrom Phong, Thong Lo, Ekkamai, Phra Khanong, On Nut, Bang Chak, Punnawithi, Udom Suk, Bang Na and Bearing.

M MRT Queen Sirikit National Convention Centre, Sukhumvit (interchange with BTS Asok) and Phetchaburi.

Neighbourhood Map on p142

Th Sukhumvit area, including Terminal 21 (p158)
ADUMM76/SHUTTERSTOCK ©

Thanon Sukhumvit

A
B
C
D

1

32 🎏

23 🎏

Soi Sawatd

Soi 3 (Nana)

17 ✕

Soi 5
Soi 7
Soi 11
Soi 13
Soi 15

Soi 21 (Asoke)

Soi 23

Soi Prasanmit

Soi 31

20 ✕

Rajawongse

2

44 ✿

Nana Ⓢ 🏧 **48**

Raja's
Fashions

Yoga Elements
Studio
⊙ **8**

Siam
Society &
Kamthieng
House

38 ⊙

Soi 19

19 ⊙

Soi 31

31 🍸

Chuvit
Garden **9** ⊙

16 ✕

1 ⊙

Sukhumvit Ⓢ

43 ✿

Divana
Massage
& Spa

13 🍸 ✕ **10**

Soi 4

Soi 8
Soi 10
Soi 12

39 ✕

46 🏧

Soi 25

Soi 27

Soi 33

Asok Ⓢ

3

Tailor
on Ten

Th Ratchadaphisek

Soi 14

Soi 16

Soi 18

Soi 20

Soi 22

Th Sukhumvit

Soi 31

Soi 31/1

Soi 33/1

29 🍸

47 🏧 Phrom
Phong Ⓢ

4

Benjakiti
Park

41 🍸
22 ✕

Benjasiri
Park

Emporium

12 🍸 **26**

Lake
Ratchada

42 ✿

Eight
Limbs **7** ✿

Phussapa
Thai Massage
School **6** ⊙

5

Benjakiti
Park **4** ⊙

Queen Sirikit
National
Convention
Centre Ⓜ

Queen Sirikit National
Convention Centre

KHLONG
TOEY

Soi 22

Soi 24

Soi 26

Khlong
Toei Ⓜ

Rama IV

6

Khlong
Toey
Market **3** ⊙

For reviews see	
⊙ Sights	p144
✕ Eating	p146
🍸 Drinking	p150
✿ Entertainment	p155
🏧 Shopping	p157

A
B
C
D

E   F   G   H

Kamphaeng Phet 7
Th Phetchaburi
1
40 ⊛▶

Khlong Saen Saeb

Soi 39

Subhashok
The Arts Centre
2

Soi 39

Soi 49

Sukhumvit 55

30
2
25

Soi Ekamai 21

Soi Phrom Si 2

Soi Prom Si 1

36

Soi 39

21

14 ⊗
35
33

Soi Thong Lor 16
Soi 49/9

Soi 63 (Ekamai)

3

Soi Thong
Lor 15

Soi Thong Lor 13

49

Soi 49

Soi Prommit

Soi 53

Soi 9

Soi 55 (Thong Lor)

Soi Thong Lor 10

37

4

Soi 39

Soi 41
Soi 43
Soi 47

Soi 49
Soi 51

Soi 53

34

Soi
Thong Lor 5

Soi Ekamai 10
Coran
27

15 ⊗

Soi 28
Soi 30

Th Sukhumvit

45
24

Soi
Thong Lor 1

11
18

Asia Herb
Association

Soi 61

Soi 63 (Ekamai)

Soi Ekamai 6

Soi Ekamai 4
5

Soi 34

Thong Lo ⓢ

Soi 59

28 ⓢ   Soi Ekamai 2

Soi 36

Soi 38

Eastern
Bus Terminal
ⓢ Ekkamai

6

⊛Ⓝ 0 ____ 500 m
0 ____ 0.25 miles

Stanley
MiniVenture
5

E   F   G   H

Sights

Siam Society & Kamthieng House

MUSEUM

1 MAP P142, B2

Kamthieng House transports visitors to a northern Thai village complete with informative displays of daily rituals, folk beliefs and everyday household chores, all within the setting of a traditional wooden house. This museum is operated by and shares space with the Siam Society, publisher of the renowned *Journal of the Siam Society* and a valiant preserver of traditional Thai culture. (สยามสมาคม & บ้านคำเที่ยง; www.siam-society.org; 131 Soi 21/Asoke, Th Sukhumvit; adult/child 100B/free; ◷9am-5pm Tue-Sat; Ⓜ Sukhumvit exit 1, Ⓢ Asok exit 3 or 6)

Decoding the Soi

All odd-numbered soi branching off Thanon Sukhumvit head north, while even numbers run south. Unfortunately, they don't line up sequentially (eg Soi 11 lies directly opposite Soi 8, Soi 39 is opposite Soi 26). Also, some larger soi are better known by alternative names, such as Soi 3/Nana Neua, Soi 21/Asoke, Soi 55/Thong Lor and Soi 63/Ekamai.

Subhashok The Arts Centre

GALLERY

2 MAP P142, E2

Tucked deep in a residential Th Sukhumvit side street is this vast new gallery, a collaboration with Paris' Galerie Adler and one of the city's most ambitious art spaces. So far the artists have largely stemmed from the big-name, often politically motivated, Thai art world. (SAC; www.sac.gallery; 160/3 Soi 33, Th Sukhumvit; ◷10am-5.30pm Sat, noon-6pm Sun; Ⓢ Phrom Phong exit 6 & taxi)

Khlong Toey Market

MARKET

3 MAP P142, B6

This wholesale market, one of the city's largest, is the origin of many of the meals you'll eat during your stay in Bangkok. Get there early and bring a camera; although some corners of the market can't exactly be described as photogenic, the cheery fishmongers and stacks of durians make great happy snaps. By 10am, most vendors have already packed up and left. (ตลาดคลองเตย; cnr Th Ratchadaphisek & Rama IV; ◷5-10am; Ⓜ Khlong Toei exit 1)

Benjakiti Park

PARK

4 MAP P142, B5

This 130-*rai* (20.8-hectare) park is built on what was once a part of the Tobacco Monopoly, a vast, crown-owned expanse of low-rise factories and warehouses. There's an artificial lake that's good for jogging and cycling around its 2km track. Bikes can be **hired** (per hour 40B; ⏰8am-7pm). (สวนเบญจกิติ; Th Ratchadaphisek; ⏰5am-8pm; 🚻; Ⓜ Queen Sirikit National Convention Centre exit 3)

Stanley MiniVenture
MUSEUM

5 ◎ MAP P142, H6

Kids (and closet model-train enthusiasts) will get a kick out of this entire town in miniature. (www.stanleyminiventure.com; 2nd fl, Gateway Ekamai, 982/22 Th Sukhumvit; adult/child 500/400B; ⏰10am-8pm)

Phussapa Thai Massage School
HEALTH & WELLBEING

6 ◎ MAP P142, D4

Run by a long-time Japanese resident of Bangkok, the basic course in Thai massage here spans 30 hours over five days; there are shorter courses in foot massage and self-massage. (📞02 204 2922; www.facebook.com/phussapa; 25/8 Soi 26, Th Sukhumvit; tuition from 6000B, Thai massage per hour 250B; ⏰lessons 9am-4pm, massage 11am-11pm; Ⓢ Phrom Phong exit 4)

Eight Limbs
MARTIAL ARTS

7 ◎ MAP P142, D4

This small gym in downtown Bangkok offers 1½-hour walk-in lessons in *moo·ay tai* (Thai boxing; also spelt *muay Thai*) for all skill levels. See the Facebook page for times. (📞090 987 9590; www.facebook.com/8limbsluaythaigym; Soi 24, Th Sukhumvit; lessons from 580B; ⏰10am-8.30pm Tue-Sun; Ⓢ Phrom Phong exit 2)

Ratchada Lake, Benjakiti Park

SVETLANA GAJIC/SHUTTERSTOCK ©

Thanon Sukhumvit Sights

Ethnic Cuisine

Sukhumvit's various ethnic enclaves are the logical destination if you're growing weary of rice and spice. Known colloquially as Little Arabia, Soi 3/1 is home to several Middle Eastern restaurants, while a handful of Korean restaurants can be found at Soi 12 and several Japanese restaurants are located around BTS Phrom Phong.

Yoga Elements Studio YOGA

8 ◉ MAP P142, B2

Run by American Adrian Cox, who trained at Om in New York and who teaches primarily *vinyasa* and *ashtanga*, this is the most respected yoga studio in town. The high-rise location helps you rise above it all, too. (☏02 255 9552; www.yogaelements.com; 7th fl, 185 Dhammalert Bldg, Th Sukhumvit; classes from 600B; ⓢChit Lom exit 5)

Chuvit Garden PARK

9 ◉ MAP P142, B2

The eponymous benefactor of this park ran unsuccessfully for Bangkok's governor in 2004, and successfully for the Thai parliament in 2005 and 2011. This park was one of his early campaign promises. It's a pretty green patch in a neighbourhood lean on trees.

Yet the story behind the park is shadier than the plantings. Chuvit Kamolvisit was arrested in 2003 for illegally bulldozing, rather than legally evicting, tenants off the land where the park now stands. With all the media attention, he sang like a bird about the police bribes he handed out during his career as Bangkok's biggest massage-parlour owner, and then became an unlikely activist against police corruption. In 2016, the cops got the last laugh when Chuvit was found guilty of three different charges related to the bulldozing and was sentenced to two years in prison. (สวนชูวิทย์; Th Sukhumvit; ⏲6-10am & 4-8pm; ⓢNana exit 4)

Eating

Sri Trat THAI $$

10 ✖ MAP P142, D3

This new restaurant specialises in the unique fare of Thailand's eastern provinces, Trat and Chanthaburi. What this means is lots of rich, slightly sweet, herbal flavours, fresh seafood and dishes you won't find anywhere else in town. Highly recommended. (www.facebook.com/sritrat; 90 Soi 33, Th Sukhumvit; mains 180-450B; ⏲noon-11pm Wed-Mon; ❄; ⓢPhrom Phong exit 5)

Soul Food Mahanakorn THAI $$

11 ✖ MAP P142, F5

This contemporary staple gets its interminable buzz from its dual nature as both an inviting restaurant – the menu spans tasty interpretations of rustic Thai dishes – and a bar serving deliciously boozy, Thai-influenced cocktails. Reservations recommended. (📞 02 714 7708; www. soulfoodmahanakorn.com; 56/10 Soi 55/Thong Lor, Th Sukhumvit; mains 140-290B; ⏰ 5.30pm-midnight; ❄️ 🍴; 🚇 Thong Lo exit 3)

Jidori Cuisine Ken   JAPANESE $$

12 🔪 MAP P142, D4

This cosy Japanese restaurant does tasty tofu dishes, delicious salads and even excellent desserts; basically everything here is above average, but the highlight are the smoky, perfectly seasoned chicken skewers. Reservations recommended. (📞 02 661 3457; www. facebook.com/jidoriken; off Soi 26, Th Sukhumvit; mains 60-350B; ⏰ 5pm-midnight Mon-Sat, to 10pm Sun; ❄️; 🚇 Phrom Phong exit 4)

Appia   ITALIAN $$$

13 🔪 MAP P142, D3

Handmade pastas, slow-roasted meats and a carefully curated and relatively affordable wine list are the selling points of this restaurant serving Roman-style cuisine – for our baht, one of the best places in town for non-Thai dinner. Reservations recommended. (📞 02 261 2056; www.appia-bangkok.com; 20/4 Soi 31, Th Sukhumvit; mains 400-1000B; ⏰ 6.30-11pm Tue-Sat, 11.30am-2.30pm & 6.30-11pm Sun; ❄️ 🍴; 🚇 Phrom Phong exit 5)

The Commons   MARKET $$$

14 🔪 MAP P142, G3

Trendy Thong Lor gets even cooler with this marketplace-style eatery that is packed with reliable names such as Soul Food 555, Peppina and Meat & Bones, along with a coffee roaster, a craft-beer bar and wine vendor. It's an ideal place to idle away an evening listening to Jack Johnson wannabes strum acoustic sets. (www.thecommonsbkk. com; 335 Soi 17, Soi 55/Thong Lor, Th Sukhumvit; mains 500-2000B; ⏰ 8am-midnight; ❄️ 🍴; 🚇 Thong Lo exit 3 & taxi)

Quince   INTERNATIONAL $$$

15 🔪 MAP P142, E4

Back in 2011, Quince made an audible splash in Bangkok's dining scene with its retro/industrial interior and eclectic, internationally influenced menu. The formula has since been copied ad nauseam,

Cooking with Poo & Friends

This popular **cooking course** (📞 080 434 8686; www.cooking withpoo.com; classes 1500B; ⏰ 8.30am-1pm; 👶) was started by a native of Khlong Toey's slums and is held in her neighbourhood. Courses, which must be booked in advance, span three dishes and include a visit to Khlong Toey Market and transport to and from Emporium Shopping Centre.

> ### Smoking in Public Spaces
> Be aware that smoking has been outlawed in Bangkok at all indoor (and some quasi-outdoor) entertainment places since 2008.

but Quince continues to put out the type of vibrant, full-flavoured dishes, many with palpable Middle Eastern or Spanish influences, that made it stand out in the first place. (☏02 662 4478; www.quincebangkok.com; Soi 45, Th Sukhumvit; mains 150-3900B; ⏰11.30am-1am; ❄️🌶️; 🚇Phrom Phong exit 3)

Myeong Ga
KOREAN $$$

16 ❌ MAP P142, B2

Located on the ground floor of Sukhumvit Plaza (the multistorey complex also known as Korean Town), this restaurant is the city's best destination for authentic Seoul food. Go for the tasty prepared dishes or, if you've got a bit more time, the excellent DIY Korean-style barbecue. (ground fl, Sukhumvit Plaza, cnr Soi 12 & Th Sukhumvit; mains 200-950B; ⏰11am-10pm Tue-Sun, 4-10pm Mon; ❄️; 🚇Sukhumvit exit 3, 🚇Asok exit 2)

Daniel Thaiger
AMERICAN $$

17 ❌ MAP P142, B1

Bangkok's best burgers are served from this American-run stall that, at the time of research, had a long-standing location on Soi 11. Check

the Facebook page to see where the food truck will be when you're in town. (☏084 549 0995; www.facebook.com/danielthaiger; Soi 11, Th Sukhumvit; mains from 140B; ⏰11am-late; 🚇Nana exit 3)

Bo.lan
THAI $$$

18 ❌ MAP P142, F5

Upscale Thai is often more garnish than flavour, but Bo.lan has proved to be the exception. Bo and Dylan (Bo.lan is a play their names and means 'ancient') take a scholarly approach to Thai cuisine, and generous set meals featuring full-flavoured Thai dishes are the result of this tuition (à la carte is not available; meat-free meals are). Reservations recommended. (☏02 260 2962; www.bolan.co.th; 24 Soi 53, Th Sukhumvit; set meals 1200-3500B; ⏰6-10.30pm Tue-Sun, noon-2.30pm Sat & Sun; ❄️🌶️; 🚇Thong Lo exit 1)

Bharani
THAI $

19 ❌ MAP P142, C2

This cosy Thai restaurant dabbles in a bit of everything, from ox-tongue stew to rice fried with shrimp paste, but the real reason to come is for the rich, meaty 'boat noodles' – so called because they used to be sold from boats plying the *klorng* (canals; also spelt *khlong*) of central Thailand. (Sansab Boat Noodle; 96/14 Soi 23, Th Sukhumvit; mains 60-250B; ⏰11am-10pm; ❄️; 🚇Sukhumvit exit 2, 🚇Asok exit 3)

Nasir Al-Masri   MIDDLE EASTERN $$$

20 ❌ MAP P142, A1

One of several Middle Eastern restaurants on Soi 3/1, Nasir Al-Masri is easily recognisable by its floor-to-ceiling stainless-steel 'theme'. Middle Eastern food often means meat, meat and more meat, but the menu here also includes several delicious vegie-based *mezze* (small dishes). (4/6 Soi 3/1, Th Sukhumvit; mains 160-370B; ⏰24hr; ❄️🖊️; ⓢ Nana exit 1)

Pier 21   THAI $

Ascend a seemingly endless series of escalators to arrive at this noisy food court in the Terminal 21 shopping centre (see 46 🅐 Map p142, B3). There are offerings from vendors from across the city, so the selection is vast (and includes a large vegetarian stall). Dishes are exceedingly cheap, even by Thai standards. (5th fl; mains 40-200B)

Klang Soi Restaurant   THAI $

21 ❌ MAP P142, F3

If you had a Thai grandma who lived in the Sukhumvit area, this is where she'd eat. The mimeographed menu spans old-school specialities from central and southern Thailand, and also has as a few Western dishes. Located at the end of Soi 49/9, in the Racquet Club complex. (Soi 49/9, Th Sukhumvit; mains 80-250B; ⏰11am-2.30pm & 5-10pm Tue-Sun; ❄️; ⓢ Phrom Phong exit 3 & taxi)

Soul Food Mahanakorn (p146)

Tipping Etiquette

You shouldn't be surprised to learn that the tipping custom that is followed in Thailand is not as exact as it is in Japan (tip no one) or the USA (tip everyone). Thailand falls somewhere in between those two extremes and some areas are left open to interpretation. Some people will leave roughly 10% tip at any sit-down restaurant where someone fills their glass every time they take a sip. Others don't. Most upmarket restaurants will apply a 10% service charge to the bill. Some patrons leave extra on top of the service charge, while others do not. The choice is entirely yours.

Saras   INDIAN $

 22   MAP P142, C4

Describing your restaurant as a 'fast-food feast' may not be the cleverest PR strategy we've encountered, but it's a pretty spot-on description of this Indian restaurant. Order at the counter to be rewarded with *dosai* (crispy southern Indian bread), meat-free regional set meals or rich curries (dishes are brought to your table). We wish all fast food could be this satisfying. (www.saras.co.th; Soi 20, Th Sukhumvit; mains 90-200B; ☺9am-10.30pm; ❄🖥; Ⓜ Sukhumvit exit 2, Ⓢ Asok exit 4)

Drinking

WTF   BAR

Wonderful Thai Friendship (what did you think it stood for?) is a funky and friendly neighbourhood bar near Studio Lam (see 24 ⓖ Map p142, F5) that also packs in a gallery space. Arty locals and resident foreigners come for the old-school cocktails, live music and DJ events, poetry readings, art exhibitions and tasty bar snacks. And we, like them, give WTF our vote for Bangkok's best bar. (www.wtfbangkok.com; 7 Soi 51, Th Sukhumvit; ☺6pm-1am Tue-Sun; 📶; Ⓢ Thong Lo exit 3)

Q&A Bar   BAR

23 ⓖ MAP P142, C1

Imagine a midcentury-modern dining car or airport lounge and you're close to picturing the interior of Q&A. The short list of featured cocktails can appear to be a divergence from the classic vibe, but an old-world dress code and manners are encouraged. (www.qnabar.com; 235/13 Soi 21/Asoke, Th Sukhumvit; ☺7pm-2am Mon-Sat)

Studio Lam   BAR, CLUB

24 ⓖ MAP P142, F5

Studio Lam is an extension of uberhip record label ZudRangMa, and boasts a Jamaican-style sound system custom-built for world and retro-Thai DJ sets and the occasional live show. For a night of dancing in Bangkok that doesn't revolve around Top 40 cheese, this is the place. (www.facebook.com/studiolambangkok; 3/1 Soi 51, Th Sukhumvit; ☻6pm-1am Tue-Sun; ⑤ Thong Lo exit 3)

Tuba
BAR

25 MAP P142, H2

Part storage room for over-the-top vintage furniture, part restaurant and part friendly local boozer; this quirky bar certainly doesn't lack

in diversity – nor fun. Indulge in a whole bottle (they'll hold onto it for your next visit if you don't finish it) and don't miss the moreish chicken wings or the delicious deep-fried *lâhp* (a tart/spicy salad of minced meat). (www.facebook.com/tubabkk; 34 Room 11-12 A, Soi Thong Lor 20/Soi Ekamai 21; ☻11am-2am; ⑤ Ekkamai exit 1 & taxi)

Waon
KARAOKE

26 MAP P142, D4

Is the canned soundtrack the only thing that's preventing you from

Bangkok Taxi Alternatives

Getting burnt by taxi drivers who refuse to use the meter or take you where you want to go? Rest assured that there are alternatives to traditional taxis in Bangkok – sort of.

Uber (www.uber.com/cities/bangkok), undoubtedly the most well-known – and controversial – ride service in the world, was introduced to Thailand in 2014. It quickly gained popularity among those looking to avoid the usual Bangkok taxi headaches: communication issues, perpetual lack of change and reckless drivers. Yet in late 2014, Thailand's Department of Land Transport made the app-based outfit illegal, declaring that its vehicles weren't properly registered, its fares unregulated and its drivers unlicensed. At the time of research, the situation seemed to have reached a stalemate, with Uber still operating in Bangkok, albeit less conspicuously.

The good news is that other outfits such as **GrabTaxi** (www.grabtaxi.com/bangkok-thailand) and **Easy Taxi** (www.easytaxi.com/th), both of which operate via taxis that are already registered, haven't been affected by the ruling. And in 2015, a domestic alternative, **All Thai Taxi** (www.allthaitaxi.com), was introduced.

However, if you insist on keeping it old school, here's a Bangkok taxi tip: avoid taxis parked in front of hotels or tourist zones, who inevitably never use the meter and who tend to be selective about where they go. Instead, walk a block or so away and flag a moving taxi.

Opening Hours

Since 2004 authorities have ordered most of Bangkok's bars and clubs to close by 1am. A complicated zoning system sees venues in designated 'entertainment areas', including Th Silom and parts of Th Sukhumvit, open until 2am, but even these 'later' licences are subject to police whimsy.

obtaining karaoke superstardom? At Waon, muzak is replaced by a real live piano player. The music and clientele are predominantly Japanese, but the friendly owner is happy to play Western standards. And even if you can't sing, you can pitch in via maracas, bongos or acoustic guitar. (10/11 Soi 26, Th Sukhumvit; ⊘8pm-1am Mon-Sat)

Mikkeller   BAR

27 🚇 MAP P142, H4

These buzz-generating Danish 'gypsy' brewers have set up shop in Bangkok, granting us more than 30 beers on tap. Expect brews ranging from the local (Sukhumvit Brown Ale) to the insane (Beer Geek, a 13% alcohol oatmeal stout), as well as an inviting atmosphere and good bar snacks. (www.mikkellerbangkok.com; 26 Yaek 2, Soi Ekamai 10; ⊘5pm-midnight; ⑤Ekkamai exit 1 & taxi)

A R Sutton & Co Engineers Siam   BAR

28 🚇 MAP P142, G5

Skeins of copper tubing, haphazardly placed one-of-a-kind antiques, zinc ceiling panels, and rows of glass vials and baubles culminate in one of the most unique and beautifully fantastical bars in Bangkok – if not anywhere. An adjacent distillery provides fuel for the bar's largely gin-based cocktails. (Parklane, Soi 63/Ekamai, Th Sukhumvit; ⊘6pm-midnight; ⑤Ekkamai exit 2)

Walden   BAR

29 🚇 MAP P142, D3

Get past the hyperminimalist *Kinfolk* vibe, and the thoughtful Japanese touches of this bar make it one of the more welcoming places in town. The brief menu of drinks spans Japanese-style 'highballs', craft beers from the USA, and simple, delicious bar snacks. (7/1 Soi 31, Th Sukhumvit; ⊘6.30pm-1am Mon-Sat; ⑤Phrom Phong exit 5)

Sugar Ray   BAR

30 🚇 MAP P142, H2

Run by a team of fun and funky Thai dudes who make flavoured syrups, Sugar Ray is a fun, funky hidden bar serving fun, funky cocktails; think an Old Fashioned made with aged rum, orange and cardamom syrup, and garnished with a piece of caramelised bacon. (www.facebook.com/sugar

raybkk; off Soi Ekamai 21; ⏲8pm-2am Wed, Fri & Sat; Ⓢ Ekkamai exit 1 & taxi)

Dim Dim   BAR

31 🚇 MAP P142, D2

Bangkok's love of Chinese-themed bars reaches its zenith at Dim Dim, a candlelit cocktail bar in Phrom Phong. China's lucky colour of red dominates the decor, and a row of gold waving cats beckons you to try the house speciality chrysanthemum vodka. Sip an Oolong Tea and Orange Sour, an Asian take on the whiskey sour, made with oolong tea and orange-peel-infused bourbon. (☏02 085 2788; www.facebook.com/dimdimbarbkk; 27/1 Soi 33, Th Sukhumvit; ⏲6.30pm-1.30am Mon-Sat; Ⓢ Phrom Phong exit 5)

Havana Social Club   CLUB

32 🚇 MAP P142, A1

Locate the phone booth, dial the secret code (the doorman will help you out here) and cross the threshold to prerevolution Havana. Part bar, part dance club, Havana combines live music, great drinks and an expat-heavy crowd who all seem to know the right dance steps. A great place to escape the cheesiness and Top 40 soundtrack that dominate most Bangkok clubs. (www.facebook.com/pg/havanasocialbkk; Soi 11, Th Sukhumvit; ⏲6pm-2am)

Beam   CLUB

33 🚇 MAP P142, G3

High-profile guest DJs spinning deep house and techno, a diverse

Thai-style orange cocktail

Spa
Central

Th Sukhumvit is home to many of Bangkok's most recommended and reputable spas and massage studios, including the following:

Asia Herb Association (Map p143, F5; ☎ 02 392 3631; www.asiaherb association.com; 58/19-25 Soi 55/Thong Lor, Th Sukhumvit; Thai massage 1hr 500B, with herbal compress 1½hr 1100B; ◷9am-midnight; ⓢ Thong Lo exit 3) This chain specialises in massage using *brà·kóp*, compresses filled with 18 different herbs.

Coran (Map p143, H4; ☎ 02 726 9978; www.coranbangkok.com; 94-96/1 Soi Ekamai 10, Soi 63/Ekamai, Th Sukhumvit; Thai massage per hour from 600B; ◷11am-10pm; ⓢ Ekkamai exit 4 & taxi) A classy spa housed in a Thai villa.

Divana Massage & Spa (Map p142, C3; ☎ 02 261 6784; www.divanaspa. com; 7 Soi 25, Th Sukhumvit; massage from 1200B, spa packages from 2650B; ◷11am-11pm Mon-Fri, 10am-11pm Sat & Sun; Ⓜ Sukhumvit exit 2, ⓢ Asok exit 6) Divana retains a unique Thai touch, with a private setting in a garden house.

crowd and a dance floor that literally vibrates have combined to make Beam Bangkok's club of the moment. Check the website for special events. (www.beamclub.com; 72 Courtyard, 72 Soi 55/Thong Lor, Th Sukhumvit; ◷9pm-late Wed-Sat; ⓢ Thong Lo exit 3 & taxi)

J Boroski Mixology
BAR

34 🚇 MAP P142, G4

The eponymous mixologist here has done away with both addresses and cocktail menus to arrive at the modern equivalent of the speakeasy. Tell the boys behind the bar what flavours you fancy, and using top-shelf liquor and unique ingredients they'll create something memorable.Located in an unmarked street near Soi Thong Lor 7; refer to the website

for the exact location. (www.joseph boroski.com; off Soi 55/Thong Lor, Th Sukhumvit; ◷7pm-2am; 🛜; ⓢ Thong Lo exit 3 & taxi)

Badmotel
BAR

35 🚇 MAP P142, G3

Badmotel blends the modern and the kitschy, the cosmopolitan and the Thai, in a way that has struck a nerve among Bangkok hipsters. This is manifested in drinks that combine rum with Hale's Blue Boy, a Thai childhood drink staple, and bar snacks such as *naam prik ong* (a northern Thai–style dip), here served with papadums. (www.facebook.com/ badmotel; 331/4-5 Soi 55/Thong Lor, Th Sukhumvit; ◷5pm-1am; ⓢ Thong Lo exit 3 & taxi)

Shades of Retro
BAR

36 MAP P142, G3

As the name suggests, this eclectic place takes Bangkok's vintage fetish to the max. You'll have to wind around Vespas and Naugahyde sofas to reach your seat, but you'll be rewarded with friendly service, free popcorn and a varied domestic soundtrack (the people behind Shades also run the domestic indie label Small Room). (www.facebook.com/shadesofretrobar; Soi Thararom 2, Soi 55/Thong Lor, Th Sukhumvit; ☺5pm-2am; S Thong Lo exit 3 & taxi)

Demo
CLUB

37 MAP P142, H4

Demo combines blasting beats and a NYC warehouse vibe. Fridays and Saturdays see a 400B entrance fee for foreigners, and ID is necessary to gain entry. (www.facebook.com/demobangkok; Arena 10, Soi Thong Lor 10/Soi Ekamai 5; ☺9pm-2am; S Ekkamai exit 2 & taxi)

Glow
CLUB

38 MAP P142, C2

Pocket-sized and boasting a world-class sound system and legit underground cred, Glow is a veteran of Bangkok's dance scene. Check the Facebook page for visiting DJs and upcoming events. (www.facebook.com/GlowBkk; 96/415 Soi Prasanmit; from 350B; ☺9pm-3am Wed-Sat, to midnight Sun; M Sukhumvit exit 2, S Asok exit 3)

Sing Sing Theater
BAR

Dancers dressed in cheongsams or neon spacesuits (depending on the night) float through secret rooms, across towering platforms and onto the tiny dance floor at this wonderfully surreal bar-slash-nightclub at Quince (see 15 ✖ Map p142, E4). The strong drinks only help to heighten the feeling that you've fallen into a Chinese opium den. Check Facebook (www.facebook.com/SingSingTheater) for a list of the bar's theme nights. (www.singsingbangkok.com; ☺9pm-2am Tue-Sun; S Thong Lo exit 1)

Entertainment

The Living Room
LIVE MUSIC

39 ⭐ MAP P142, B3

Don't let looks deceive you: every night this bland hotel lounge transforms into the city's best venue for live jazz. True to the name, there's comfy, sofa-based seating, all of it within earshot of the music. Enquire ahead of time to see which

Club Alley

The streets that extend from Th Sukhumvit are home to many of Bangkok's most popular clubs. Ravers of university age tend to head to Soi 63/Ekamai, while the pampered elite play at Soi 55/Thong Lor, and expats and tourists tend to gravitate towards the clubs on Soi 11.

Bangkok's Savile Row

The strip of Th Sukhumvit between the BTS stops of Nana and Asok is home to some of Bangkok's most famous tailors.

Tailor on Ten (Map p142, A3; ☎ 084 877 1543; www.tailoronten.com; 93 Soi 8, Th Sukhumvit; ⊙ 9.30am-7pm Mon-Sat) Set prices, foreign management and, most importantly, good tailoring, have earned this outfit heaps of praise and repeat customers.

Raja's Fashions (Map p142, A2; ☎ 02 253 8379; www.rajasfashions. com; 160/1 Th Sukhumvit; ⊙ 10.30am-8pm Mon-Sat; Ⓢ Nana exit 4) With his photographic memory for names, Bobby will make you feel as important as the long list of VIPs he has fitted over the decades that he has worked in the tailoring business.

Rajawongse (Map p142, A2; ☎ 02 255 3714; www.dress-for-success.com; 130 Th Sukhumvit; ⊙ 10.30am-8pm Mon-Sat; Ⓢ Nana exit 2) Jesse and Victor's creations are renowned among American visitors and residents.

sax master or hide-hitter is in town. An entry fee of 300B is charged after 8.30pm. (☎ 02 649 8888; www.thelivingroomatbangkok.com; level 1, Sheraton Grande Sukhumvit, 250 Th Sukhumvit; ⊙ 6pm-midnight; Ⓜ Sukhumvit exit 3, Ⓢ Asok exit 2)

Lam Sing
LIVE MUSIC

40 ✪ MAP P142, H1

Even Ziggy Stardust–era David Bowie has nothing on this dark, decadent, rhinestone-encrusted den, one of Bangkok's best venues for *mǒr lam* and *lôok tûng,* music with roots in Thailand's rural northeast. Come for raucous live-music performances accompanied by tightly choreographed, flagrantly costumed backup dancers.There's no English-language sign here, but most taxi drivers are familiar with the place. (อีสานลำซิ่ง; www.facebook.

com/isanlamsing; 57/5 Th Phet Phra Ram; ⊙ 9.30pm-4am; Ⓢ Ekkamai exit 1 & taxi)

Titanium
LIVE MUSIC

41 ✪ MAP P142, C3

Many come to this cheesy 'ice bar' for the chill, the skimpily dressed working girls and the flavoured vodka, but we come for Unicorn, the all-female house band, who rock the house from Monday to Saturday. (www.titaniumbangkok. com; 2/30 Soi 22, Th Sukhumvit; ⊙ 8pm-1am; Ⓢ Phrom Phong exit 6)

Friese-Greene Club
CINEMA

42 ✪ MAP P142, C4

You couldn't find a bigger contrast with Bangkok's huge, mall-bound cinemas than this private theatre with just nine seats. Check the website for a schedule of upcoming films. (FGC; ☎087 000 0795; www.fgc.in.th; 259/6 Soi 22, Th Sukhumvit; S Phrom Phong exit 6)

Soi Cowboy
RED-LIGHT DISTRICT

43 ⭐ MAP P142, C3

This single-lane strip of raunchy bars claims direct lineage to the post–Vietnam War R&R era. A real flesh trade functions amid the flashing neon. (Soi Cowboy; ⌚4pm-2am; M Sukhumvit exit 2, S Asok exit 3)

Nana Entertainment Plaza
RED-LIGHT DISTRICT

44 ⭐ MAP P142, A2

Nana is a three-storey go-go bar complex where the sexpats are separated from the gawking tourists. It's also home to a few *gà·teu·i*

(cross-dresser or transgender; also spelt *kàthoey*) bars. (Soi 4, Th Sukhumvit; ⌚4pm-2am; S Nana exit 2)

Shopping

ZudRangMa Records
MUSIC

45 🔒 MAP P142, F5

The headquarters of this retro/ world label is a chance to finally combine the university-era pastimes of record-browsing and drinking. Come to snicker at corny old Thai vinyl covers or invest in some of the label's highly regarded compilations of classic *mǒr lam* and *lôok tûng* (Thai-style country music). (www.zudrangmarecords.com; 7/1 Soi 51, Th Sukhumvit; ⌚2-9pm Tue-Sun; S Thong Lo exit 1)

Soi Cowboy

Terminal 21   SHOPPING CENTRE

46 🔒 MAP P142, B3

Catering to an innate Thai need for wacky objects to be photographed in front of, this huge mall is worth a visit for the spectacle as much as the shopping. Start at the basement-level 'airport' and proceed upwards through 'Paris', 'Tokyo' and other city-themed floors. Who knows, you might even buy something. (www.terminal21.co.th; cnr Th Sukhumvit & Soi 21/Asoke; ⏱10am-10pm; Ⓜ Sukhumvit exit 3, Ⓢ Asok exit 3)

Emquartier   SHOPPING CENTRE

47 🔒 MAP P142, D4

One of Bangkok's newest malls and arguably its flashiest. Come for brands you're not likely to find elsewhere, or get lost in the Helix, a seemingly never-ending spiral of more than 50 restaurants. (www.theemdistrict.com; 693-695 Th Sukhumvit; ⏱10am-10pm; Ⓢ Phrom Phong exit 1)

Thanon Sukhumvit Market   GIFTS & SOUVENIRS

48 🔒 MAP P142, A2

Knock-off clothes and watches, stacks of skin-flick DVDs, Chinese throwing stars and other questionable gifts perfect for your teenage brother dominate this market catering to package and sex tourists. (btwn Soi 3 & Soi 15, Th Sukhumvit; ⏱11am-11pm Tue-Sun; Ⓢ Nana exits 1 & 3)

Emquartier

NATTAKIT JEERAPATMAITREE/SHUTTERSTOCK ©

Quartor
FASHION & ACCESSORIES

Taking up nearly an entire floor in Emquartier (see 47 🔒 Map p142, D4) is this zone dedicated entirely to the works of Thai designers. Almost exclusively a female affair, the looks range from conservative to outrageous and span all the top Thai labels. (2nd fl, Bldg C; ⊙10am-10pm)

Another Story
HOMEWARES

A self-proclaimed 'lifestyle concept store' located on the fourth floor of Emquartier (see 47 🔒 Map p142, D4), Another Story is probably more accurately described as an engaging assemblage of cool stuff. Even if you're not planning to buy, it's fun to flip through the unique, domestically made items such as ceramics from Prempacha in Chiang Mai, leather goods from brands like labrador, and fragrant soaps, oils and candles from BsaB. (⊙10am-10pm)

Duly
CLOTHING

49 🔒 MAP P142, F3

High-quality Italian fabrics and experienced tailors make Duly one of the best places in Bangkok to commission a sharp shirt. (☎02 662 6647; www.laladuly.co.th; Soi 49, Th Sukhumvit; ⊙10am-7pm; Ⓢ Phrom Phong exit 1)

Sop Moei Arts
ARTS & CRAFTS

The Bangkok showroom of this nonprofit organisation features the vibrant cloth creations of Karen weavers from Mae Hong Son, in northern Thailand.It's located at the end of Soi 49/9, in the Racquet Club complex (see 21 ✖ Map p142, F3). (www.sopmoeiarts.com; ⊙9.30am-5pm Tue-Sat)

Top Sight 🛍
Chatuchak Weekend Market

Imagine all of Bangkok's markets fused together in a seemingly never-ending commerce-themed barrio. Now add a little artistic flair, a sauna-like climate and bargaining crowds and you've got a rough sketch of Chatuchak (also spelled 'Jatujak' or nicknamed 'JJ'). Once you're deep in its bowels, it will seem like there is no order and no escape, but Chatuchak is actually arranged into relatively coherent sections.

ตลาดนัดจตุจักร

www.chatuchakmarket.org

587/10 Th Phahonyothin

⏱ 7am-6pm Wed & Thu plants only, 6pm-midnight Fri wholesale only, 9am-6pm Sat & Sun

Ⓜ Chatuchak Park exit 1, Kamphaeng Phet exits 1 & 2, Ⓢ Mo Chit exit 1

Antiques, Handicrafts & Souvenirs

Section 1 is the place to go for Buddha statues, old LPs and random antiques. More secular arts and crafts, like musical instruments and hill-tribe items, can be found in Sections 25 and 26.

Art

Section 7 is a virtual open-air contemporary art gallery, where orks span the spectrum of media, and stalls are frequently changing hands.

Clothing & Accessories

Clothing dominates much of Chatuchak, starting in Section 8 and continuing through the even-numbered sections to 24. Sections 5 and 6 deal in used clothing for every Thai youth subculture, from punks to cowboys; Soi 7, where it transects Sections 12 and 14, is heavy on hip hop and skate fashions. Tourist-sized clothes and textiles are found in sections 8 and 10.

Sections 2 and 3, particularly the tree-lined Soi 2 of the former, is the Siam Sq of Chatuchak, and is home to heaps of trendy independent labels. Moving north, Soi 4 in Section 4 boasts several shops selling locally designed T-shirts.

Housewares & Decor

The western edge of the market, particularly sections 8 to 26, features all manner of housewares, from cheap plastic buckets to expensive brass woks. This area is a particularly good place to stock up on inexpensive Thai ceramics, ranging from celadon to the traditional rooster-themed bowls from Lampang.

★ Top Tips

o Schematic maps are located throughout Chatuchak; if you need more detail (not to mention insider tips), consider purchasing **Nancy Chandler's Map of Bangkok** (www.nancychandler.net), available at most Bangkok bookshops.

o Arrive at Chatuchak early – ideally around 9am or 10am – to beat the crowds and heat.

✕ Take a Break

o If you need to escape the crowds, cross Th Kamphaengphet 1 to the food court at Or Tor Kor Market (p162).

o If you're in the heart of the market and need a cold beer, consider a pit stop at Viva's (p162).

Pets

Possibly the most fun you'll ever have window-shopping will be petting puppies and cuddling kittens in Sections 13 and 15. Soi 9 of the former features several shops that deal solely in clothing for pets.

Plants & Gardening

The interior perimeter of sections 2 to 4 features a huge variety of potted plants, flowers, herbs and fruits, and the accessories needed to maintain them. Some of these shops are also open on weekday afternoons.

Eating

Lots of Thai-style eating and snacking will stave off Chatuchak rage (cranky behaviour brought on by dehydration or hunger), and numerous food stalls are set up throughout the market, particularly between Sections 6 and 8.

Drinking

Viva 8 (www.facebook.com/Viva8JJ; Section 8, Stall 371, mains 150-300B; ⏰9am-10pm Sat & Sun) features a bar, a DJ and, when we stopped by, a Spanish chef making huge platters of paella. As evening draws near, down a beer at **Viva's** (Section 26, Stall 161, ⏰10am-10pm Sat & Sun), a cafe-bar that features live music and stays open late.

Nearby: Or Tor Kor Market

Or Tor Kor Market (องค์กรตลาด เพื่อเกษตรกร; Th Kamphaengphet 1; ⏰8am-6pm; Ⓜ Kamphaeng Phet exit 3) is Bangkok's highest-quality

Bargaining

Many of your purchases at Chatuchak Weekend Market will involve an ancient skill that has long been abandoned in the West: bargaining. Contrary to what you may have seen elsewhere, bargaining is not a terse exchange of numbers and animosity. Rather, bargaining Thai style is a generally friendly transaction where two people try to agree on a price that is fair to both of them.

The first rule of bargaining is to have a general idea of the price. Ask around at a few vendors to get a rough notion. When you're ready to buy, it's generally a good strategy to start at 50% of the asking price. If you're buying several of an item, you have much more leverage to request a lower price. If the seller immediately agrees to your first price, you're probably paying too much, but it's bad form to bargain further at this point. Keeping a friendly, flexible demeanour throughout the transaction will almost always work in your favour.

fresh market, and taking in sights such as toddler-sized mangoes and dozens of pots full of curries amounts to culinary trainspotting. Head to the market at lunchtime for its open-air food court, which features dishes from across Thailand. It's directly across Th Kamphaengphet from Chatuchak Weekend Market.

Nearby: Chatuchak Park

Chatuchak Park (สวนจตุจักร; Th Phahonyothin; admission free; ⏱4.30am-9pm; Ⓜ Chatuchak Park exit 1, Kamphaeng Phet exits 1 & 2, Ⓢ Mo Chit exit 1 & 3), the weekend market's namesake, is the adjacent, tidy green space – actually a merger of three separate parks – with museums, an artificial lake and bicycles to hire.

Worth a Trip 👀
Ko Kret

Bangkok's easiest green getaway, Ko Kret is an artificial 'island', the result of a canal being dug nearly 300 years ago to shorten an oxbow bend in Mae Nam Chao Phraya. The island is one of Thailand's oldest settlements of Mon people, who were a dominant tribe of central Thailand between the 6th and 10th centuries AD. Today, Ko Kret is known for its rural atmosphere, distinctive pottery and busy weekend market.

Ko Kret is in Nonthaburi, about 15km north of central Bangkok.

🚌 Take bus 166 from the Victory Monument or a taxi to Pak Kret before boarding the cross-river ferry (2B, 5am to 9pm) that leaves from Wat Sanam Neua.

Wat Poramai Yikawat

Across from Ko Kret's main pier, **Wat Poramai Yikawat** (วัดปรมัยยิกาวาส; Ko Kret, Nonthaburi; ⊙9am-5pm; 🚌166 & river-crossing ferry from Wat Sanam Neua), has a Mon-style marble Buddha and a **museum** (admission free; ⊙1-4pm Mon-Fri, 9am-5pm Sat & Sun; 🚌166 & cross-river ferry from Wat Sanam Neua) with religious objects and exhibits on local pottery. But the temple's most famous landmark is undoubtedly the 200-year-old leaning stupa that juts out from the island's northeastern corner.

Pottery

Ko Kret is known for its hand-thrown terracotta pots, sold at markets throughout Bangkok; order an iced coffee from just about any vendor on the island and you'll get a small one as a souvenir. From Wat Poramai Yikawat, go in either direction to find both abandoned kilns and working pottery centres on the east and north coasts.

Touring the Island

A 6km paved path circles Ko Kret, and can be easily completed on foot or by bicycle, the latter available for rent from the pier (40B per day). Alternatively, it's possible to charter a boat for up to 10 people for 500B; the typical island tour stops at a batik workshop, a sweets factory and, on weekends, a floating market.

★ Top Tips

○ Ko Kret can be horribly crowded on weekends; arrive on a weekday instead. There are fewer eating and shopping options, but you'll have the place to yourself.

✗ Take a Break

The northern coast of Ko Kret is home to a row of open-air restaurants, many serving *kôw châa*, an unusual but delicious Mon dish of savoury titbits served with chilled fragrant rice. **Pa Ka Lung** (Restaurant River Side; Ko Kret; mains 30-60B; ⊙8am-4pm Mon-Fri, to 6pm Sat & Sun; 🚌166 & river-crossing ferry from Wat Sanam Neua), an open-air food court with an English-language menu and sign, serves *khâw châa* and other Thai dishes.

Worth a Trip 🔭

Ayuthaya

Ancient ruins, a rural Thai vibe, tasty food, good-value accommodation – and all of this only an hour from Bangkok. Ayuthaya was the capital of Siam from 1350. It was also a major trading port; international merchants visited and were left in awe by the temples and treasure-laden palaces. The glory lasted until 1767, when an invading Burmese army sacked the city, looting most of its treasures. In 1991 Ayuthaya's ruins were designated a Unesco World Heritage Site.

Ayuthaya is about 70km north of Bangkok.

อุทยานประวัติศาสตร์อยุธยา

individual sites 20-50B, day pass 220B

🕐 8am-5pm

Ayutthaya Tourist Center

The **Tourist Center** (ศูนย์ท่องเที่ยวอยุธยา; ☎035 246076; off Th Si Sanphet; admission free; ⏱8.30am-4.30pm) should be your first stop in Ayutthaya, as the excellent upstairs exhibition hall puts everything in context and describes the city's erstwhile glories. Also upstairs is the tiny but interesting Ayutthaya National Art Museum. Downstairs, the TAT office has lots of maps and good advice.

Ayuthaya Historical Park

The ruins of the former capital, **Ayuthaya Historical Park**, are one of Thailand's biggest tourist sites. They're separated into two distinct districts: the ruins 'on the island' in the central part of town are most easily visited by bicycle or motorbike; those 'off the island', opposite the river from the centre, are best visited by way of an evening boat tour. Notable ruins 'on the island' include Wat Mahathat and Wat Phra Si Sanphet. 'Off the island', make sure you don't miss Wat Chai Wattanaram (pictured left).

Chao Sam Phraya National Museum

The largest **museum** (พิพิธภัณฑสถานแห่งชาติเจ้า สามพระยา; ☎035 244570; cnr Th Rotchana & Th Si Sanphet; adult/child 150B/free; ⏱9am-4pm Wed-Sun; P) in the city has 2400 items on show, ranging from a 2m-high bronze-cast Buddha head to glistening treasures found in the crypts of Wat Phra Mahathat and Wat Ratburana.

Baan Hollanda

This **institution** (บ้านฮอลันดา; ☎035 245683; www.baanhollanda.org; Soi Khan Rua, Mu 4; 50B; ⏱9am-5pm Wed-Sun; P), a bright and beautifully curated 'Dutch House', features an excellent exhibition of Thai-Dutch history alongside the excavated foundations of centuries-old Dutch buildings. The Dutch East India Company (VOC) arrived in Ayutthaya in 1604 and set up a trading post here, hoping to use Thailand (then Siam) as a gateway to China.

★ Top Tips

Although buses and trains also link Bangkok and Ayutthaya, minivans are the quickest and most efficient method of reaching the city.

✗ Take a Break

Try Ayuthaya's signature dish, gǒo·ay ɗěe·o reu·a, aka 'boat noodles', so-called because they were formerly sold from boats, at **Lung Lek** (Th Chee Kun; mains 30-50B; ⏱8.30am-4pm), located conveniently across from Wat Ratburana in the historical park.

Survival Guide

BTS (Skytrain) p172 TAMANKUNG/SHUTTERSTOCK ©

Before You Go

Book Your Stay

o Bangkok is home to so many hotels that, apart from some of the smaller, boutique places, booking ahead isn't generally required.

o The cheapest hostels and guesthouses often share bathrooms and may not even supply a towel.

o Some budget places remain fan-cooled or, in the case of dorms, will only run the air-con between certain hours.

o If on offer, breakfast at most Bangkok hostels and budget hotels is little more than instant coffee and toast.

o Wi-fi is nearly universal across the spectrum, but air-conditioning and lifts are not.

o The more thoughtful top-end places have amenities such as en suite, computers and free wi-fi; in other places, it's not uncommon to have to pay a premium for wi-fi.

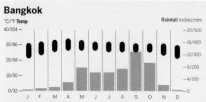

Bangkok

When to Go

o **Winter (late Dec–early Jan)** This is both the coolest time of the year in Bangkok and the peak tourist season. Consider November or February for similarly cool weather and few people.

o **Wet season (May–Oct)** During the monsoon period, Bangkok receives as much as 300mm of rain per month. The good news is that the downpours are usually brief and tourist numbers are low.

o Pools are almost standard at Bangkok's top-end hotels, not to mention fitness and business centres, restaurants and bars.

Best Budget

Lub*d (www.lubd.com) Youthful-feeling hostel with two convenient locations in central Bangkok.

Chern (www.chern bangkok.com) Surprisingly sophisticated dorms and rooms for the price.

S-Box (www.sbox hotel.com) Contemporary budget accommodation.

Niras Bangkoc (www.nirasbangkoc.com) Dorms with an old-school feel.

Best Midrange

Smile Society (www.smilesocietyhostel.com) A homey haven in the middle of Bangkok's financial district.

Feung Nakorn Balcony (www.feung nakorn.com) Former school turned cute midranger.

Tints of Blue (www.tintsofblue.com) Heavy on the charm, easy on the wallet.

Lamphu Treehouse (www.lamphutree

hotel.com) Despite the name, this attractive midranger has its feet firmly on land.

Best Top End

Metropolitan by COMO (www.como hotels.com/metro politanbangkok) Urban sophistication and excellent dining.

Mandarin Oriental (www.mandarinorien tal.com/luxury-hotel/ bangkok) Bangkok's oldest hotel remains one of its best.

Peninsula Hotel (www.bangkok.pen insula.com) Sky-high standards of service.

AriyasomVilla (www.ariyasom.com) Beautifully renovated 1940s-era villa that's one of the city's worst-kept accommodation secrets.

Useful Websites

Agoda (www.agoda. com/city/bangkok -th.html) Asia-based hotel-booking site that offers a lowest-price guarantee.

Lonely Planet (www. lonelyplanet.com/ thailand/bangkok/ hotels) Find reviews and make bookings.

Travelfish (www. travelfish.org/ country/thailand) Independent reviews with lots of reader feedback.

Arriving in Bangkok

Suvarnabhumi International Airport

Located 30km east of central Bangkok, **Suvarnabhumi International Airport** (02 132 1888; www. suvarnabhumiairport.com) began commercial international and domestic service in 2006. The airport's name is pronounced *sù·wan·ná·poom*, and it inherited the airport code (BKK) previously held by the old airport at Don Mueang. The airport website has real-time details of arrivals and departures.

Don Mueang International Airport

Bangkok's other airport, **Don Mueang**

International Airport (02 535 2111; www.don mueangairportthai.com), 25km north of central Bangkok, was retired from service in 2006 only to reopen later as the city's de facto budget hub. Terminal 1 handles international flights, while Terminal 2 is for domestic destinations.

Hualamphong Station

The city's main train terminus is known as **Hualamphong** (02 220 4334, call centre 1690; www.railway.co.th; off Rama IV; Ⓜ Hua Lamphong exit 2). It's advisable to ignore all touts here and avoid the travel agencies. To check timetables and prices for destinations, check out the website of the State Railway of Thailand (www. railway.co.th/main/ index_en.html).

Northern & Northeastern Bus Terminal

The **Northern & North-eastern Bus Terminal** (Mo Chit; northeastern routes 02 936 2852, ext 602/605, northern routes

02 936 2841, ext 325/614; Th Kamphaengphet; Kamphaeng Phet exit 1 & taxi, Mo Chit exit 3 & taxi) is located just north of Chatuchak Park. This hectic bus station is also commonly called *kǒn sòng mǒr chít* (Mo Chit station) – not to be confused with Mo Chit BTS station. Buses depart from here for all northern and northeastern destinations, as well as regional international destinations including Pakse (Laos), Phnom Penh (Cambodia), Siem Reap (Cambodia) and Vientiane (Laos). To reach the bus station, take BTS to Mo Chit or MRT to Kamphaeng Phet and transfer onto city bus 3, 77 or 509, or hop on a taxi or motorcycle taxi.

Eastern Bus Terminal

The **Eastern Bus Terminal** (☎02 391 2504; Soi 40, Th Sukhumvit; §Ekkamai exit 2) is the departure point for buses to Pattaya, Rayong, Chanthaburi and other points east, except for the border crossing at Aranya Prathet. Most people call it *sà·tǎh·nee èk·gà·mai* (Ekamai station). It's near the Ekkamai BTS station.

Southern Bus Terminal

The **Southern Bus Terminal** (Sai Tai Mai; ☎02 422 4444, call centre 1490; Th Boromaratchachonanee), commonly called *sǎi đâi mài*, lies a long way west of the centre of Bangkok. Besides serving as the departure point for all buses to destinations south of Bangkok, transport to Kanchanaburi and western Thailand also departs from here. The easiest way to reach the station is by taxi, or you can take bus 79, 159, 201 or 516 from Th Ratchadamnoen Klang.

Getting Around

BTS & MRT

o The elevated **BTS** (Skytrain; ☎02 617 6000, tourist information 02 617 7341; www.bts.co.th), also known as the Skytrain (*rót fai fáa*), whisks you through 'new' Bangkok (Silom, Sukhumvit and Siam Sq). The interchange between the two lines is at Siam station and trains run frequently from 6am to midnight. Fares range from 16B to 44B or 140B for a one-day pass. Most ticket machines only accept coins, but change is available at the information booths.

o Bangkok's Metro, the **MRT** (☎02 354 2000; www.bangkokmetro.co.th) is most helpful for people staying in the Sukhumvit or Silom area to reach the train station at Hualamphong. Fares cost from 16B to 42B or 120B for a one-day pass. The trains run frequently from 6am to midnight.

Taxi

o Although many first-time visitors are hesitant to use them, in general Bangkok's taxis are new and comfortable and the drivers are courteous and helpful, making them an excellent way to get around.

All taxis are required to use their meters, which start at 35B, and fares to most places within central Bangkok cost 60B to 90B. Freeway tolls – 25B to 70B depending on where you start – must be paid by the passenger.

Taxi Radio (✆1681; www.taxiradio.co.th) and other 24-hour 'phone-a-cab' services are available for 20B above the metered fare.

If you leave something in a taxi your best chance of getting it back (still pretty slim) is to call 1644.

Boat

River Ferries

The **Chao Phraya Express Boat** (✆02 623 6001; www.chaophraya expressboat.com) operates the main ferry service along Mae Nam Chao Phraya. The central pier is known as Tha Sathon, Saphan Taksin or sometimes Sathon/Central Pier, and connects to the BTS at Saphan Taksin station.

Boats run from 6am to 8pm. You can buy tickets (10B to 40B) at the pier or on board; hold on to your ticket as proof of purchase (an occasional formality).

The most common boats are the orange-flagged express boats. These run between Wat Rajsingkorn, south of Bangkok, to Nonthaburi, north, stopping at most major piers (15B, frequent from 6am to 7pm).

A blue-flagged tourist boat (40B, every 30 minutes from 9.30am to 5pm) runs from Sathon/Central Pier to Phra Athit/Banglamphu Pier, with stops at eight major sightseeing piers and a barely comprehensible English-language commentary. Vendors at Sathon/Central Pier tout a 150B all-day pass, but unless you plan on doing a lot of boat travel, it's not great value.

There are also dozens of cross-river ferries, which charge 3B and run every few minutes until late at night.

Private long-tail boats can be hired for sightseeing trips at Phra Athit/Banglamphu Pier, Chang Pier, Tien Pier and Oriental Pier.

Klorng Boats

Canal taxi boats run along Khlong Saen Saep (Banglamphu to Ramkhamhaeng) and are an easy way to get between Banglamphu and Jim Thompson House, the Siam Sq shopping centres (get off at Sapan Hua Chang Pier for both) and other points further east along Th Sukhumvit – after a mandatory change of boat at Pratunam Pier.

These boats are mostly used by daily commuters and pull into the piers for just a few seconds – jump straight on or you'll be left behind.

Fares range from 9B to 19B and boats run from 5.30am to 7.15pm from Monday to Friday, from 6am to 6.30pm on Saturday and from 6am to 6pm on Sunday.

Motorcycle Taxi

Motorcycle taxis (known as *motorsai*) serve two purposes in Bangkok. Most commonly and popularly they form an integral part of the public transport network, running from the corner of a main thoroughfare, such as Th Sukhumvit, to the far ends of sois (lanes) that run off that thoroughfare. Riders wear coloured, numbered vests and gather at either end of their soi, usually charging 10B to 20B for the trip (without a helmet unless you ask).

o Their other purpose is as a means of beating the traffic. You tell your rider where you want to go, negotiate a price (from 20B for a short trip up to about 150B going across town), strap on the helmet (they will insist for longer trips) and say a prayer to any god you're into.

Túk-túk

o Bangkok's iconic túk-túk (pronounced *dúk dúk*; a type of motorised rickshaw) are used by Thais for short hops not worth paying the taxi flagfall for. For foreigners, however, these emphysema-inducing machines are part of the Bangkok experience, so despite the fact that they overcharge outrageously and you can't see anything due to the low roof, pretty much

everyone takes a túk-túk at least once.

o Túk-túk are notorious for taking little 'detours' to commission-paying gem and silk shops and massage parlours. En route to 'special' temples, you'll meet 'helpful' locals who will steer you to even more rip-off opportunities. Ignore anyone offering too-good-to-be-true 20B trips.

o The vast majority of túk-túk drivers ask too much from tourists (expat *fa-ràng* never use them). Expect to be quoted a 100B fare, if not more, for even the shortest trip. Try bargaining them down to about 60B for a short trip, preferably at night when the pollution (hopefully) won't be quite so bad. Once you've done it, you'll find taxis are cheaper, cleaner, cooler and quieter.

Bus

o Bangkok's public buses are run by the **Bangkok Mass Transit Authority** (☏ 02 246 0973, call centre 1348; www.bmta.co.th).

o As the routes are not always clear, and with

Bangkok taxis being such a good deal, you'd really have to be pinching pennies to rely on buses as a way to get around Bangkok.

o Air-con bus fares range from 10B to 23B and fares for fan-cooled buses start at 6.50B.

o Most of the bus lines run between 5am and 10pm or 11pm, except for the 'all-night' buses, which run from 3am or 4am to midmorning.

o You'll most likely require the help of thinknet's *Bangkok Bus Guide*. Alternatively, you can download Transit Bangkok's guide to all the city's public transport including bus, MRT, BTS and boats at www.transitbangkok.com.

Essential Information

Business Hours

Banks and government offices close for national holidays. Some bars and clubs close during elections and certain holidays when alcohol sales are banned. Shopping centres have banks that open late.

Banks 8.30am-3.30pm; 24hr ATMs

Bars 6pm-midnight or 1am

Clubs 8pm-2am

Government Offices 8.30am-4.30pm Monday to Friday; some close for lunch

Restaurants 8am-10pm

Shops 10am-7pm

Electricity

Type A
220V/50Hz

Type C
220V/50Hz

Emergency

o The police contact number ☏191 functions as the de facto universal emergency number in Thailand and can also be used to call an ambulance or report a fire.

o The best way to deal with most problems requiring police (usually a rip-off or theft) is to contact the **tourist police** (☏nationwide 1155), who are used to dealing with foreigners and can be very helpful in the event you are arrested.

Money

Currency

The basic unit of Thai currency is the baht. There are 100 satang in one baht – though the only place you'll be able to spend them is in the ubiquitous 7-Elevens. Coins come in denominations of 25 satang, 50 satang, 1B, 2B, 5B and 10B. Paper currency comes in denominations of 20B (green), 50B (blue), 100B (red), 500B (purple) and 1000B (beige).

ATMs

Debit and ATM cards issued by a bank in your own country can be used at ATMs around Thailand to withdraw cash (in Thai baht only) directly from your account back home. ATMs are widespread throughout the country and can be relied on for the bulk of your spending cash. Most ATMs allow a maximum of 20,000B in withdrawals per day.

The downside is that Thai ATMs charge a 200B

foreign-transaction fee on top of whatever currency conversion and out-of-network fees your home bank charges. Before leaving home, shop around for a bank account that has free international ATM usage and reimburses fees incurred at other institutions' ATMs.

Credit & Debit Cards

Credit cards as well as debit cards can be used for purchases at some shops, hotels and restaurants. The most commonly accepted cards are Visa and MasterCard. American Express is typically only accepted at high-end hotels and restaurants.

Contact your bank and your credit-card provider before you leave home and notify them of your upcoming trip so that your accounts aren't suspended due to suspicious overseas activity.

To report a lost or stolen credit/debit card, call the following hotlines in Bangkok:

American Express (☏ 02 273 5544)

MasterCard (☏ 001 800 11887 0663)

Visa (☏ 001 800 11 535 0660)

Changing Money

Banks or private money changers offer the best foreign-exchange rates. When buying baht, US dollars is the most accepted currency, followed by British pounds and euros. Most banks charge a commission and duty for each travellers cheque cashed. Current exchange rates are posted at exchange counters.

Tipping

Tipping is not generally expected in Thailand, though it is appreciated. The exception is loose change from a large restaurant bill – if a meal costs 488B and you pay with a 500B note, some Thais will leave the 12B change. At many hotel restaurants or other upmarket eateries, a 10% service charge will be added to your bill.

Public Holidays

Government offices and banks close their doors on the following public holidays. For the precise dates of lunar holidays, see the Events & Festivals page of the Tourism Authority of Thailand's website (www.tourismthailand.org/Events-and-Festivals).

1 January
New Year's Day

February
(date varies) Makha Bucha Day, Buddhist holy day

6 April
Chakri Day, commemorating the founder of the Chakri dynasty, Rama I

13–15 April
Songkran Festival, traditional Thai New Year and water festival

1 May
Labour Day

5 May
Coronation Day

May/June
(date varies) Visakha Bucha, Buddhist holy day

July/August
(date varies) Asanha Bucha, Buddhist holy day

28 July
Maha Vajiralongkorn's Birthday

12 August
Queen Sirikit's Birthday/Mother's Day

23 October
Chulalongkorn Day

5 December
Commemoration of Late King Bhumiphol/Father's Day

10 December
Constitution Day

31 December
New Year's Eve

Safe Travel

Gem scam We're begging you – if you aren't a gem trader, then don't buy unset stones in Thailand. Period.

Closed today Ignore any 'friendly' local who tells you that an attraction is closed for a Buddhist holiday or for cleaning.

Túk-túk rides for 20B These alleged 'tours' bypass the sights and instead cruise to all the fly-by-night gem and tailor shops that pay commissions.

Flat-fare taxi ride Flatly refuse any driver who quotes a flat fare, which will usually be three times more

expensive than the reasonable meter rate.

Friendly strangers Be wary of smartly dressed men who approach you asking where you're from and where you're going.

Telephone
Mobile Phones

The easiest phone option in Thailand is to acquire a mobile (cell) phone equipped with a local SIM card. Buying a prepaid SIM is as simple as finding a 7-Eleven. SIM cards include talk and data packages and you can add more funds with a prepaid reload card.

Thailand is on the GSM network and mobile phone providers include AIS (1 2 Call), DTAC and True Move, all of which operate on a 4G network. Coverage and quality of the different carriers varies from year to year based on network upgrades and capacity. Carriers usually sell talk-data packages based on usage amounts.

The main networks:
AIS (1 2 Call; www.ais.co.th/12call/th)

DTAC (www.dtac.co.th)

TrueMove (www.truemove.com)

Making International & Domestic Calls

If you want to call an international number from a telephone in Thailand, you must first dial an international access code plus the country code followed by the subscriber number.

In Thailand there are various international access codes charging different rates per minute. The standard direct-dial prefix is 001; it is operated by CAT and is considered to have the best sound quality. It connects to the largest number of countries, but is also the most expensive. The next best is 007, a prefix operated by TOT with reliable quality and slightly cheaper rates. Economy rates are available through different carriers – do an internet search to determine promotion codes.

Dial 100 for operator-assisted

Dos & Don'ts

Bangkokians are generally very understanding and hospitable, but there are some important taboos and social conventions to be aware of.

Monarchy Never make any disparaging remarks about any member of Thailand's royal family. Treat objects depicting the king (such as money) with respect.

Temples Wear clothing that covers you to your knees and elbows. Remove your shoes when you enter a temple building. Sit with your feet tucked behind you to avoid pointing the bottom of your feet at Buddha images. Women should never touch a monk or a monk's belongings; step out of a monk's way on footpaths and don't sit next to a monk on public transport.

Save Face Never get into an argument with a Thai. It is better to smile through any social friction.

international calls or reverse-charge (collect) calls.

Inside Thailand all telephone numbers include an initial 0 plus the area code and the subscriber number. The only time you drop the initial 0 is when you're calling from outside Thailand.

Useful Numbers

Thailand country code ☏ 66

Bangkok area code ☏ 02

Operator-assisted international calls ☏ 100

Free local directory assistance ☏ 1133

Toilets

Increasingly, the Asian-style squat toilet is less of the norm in Thailand. There are still specimens in rural places, provincial bus stations, older homes and modest restaurants, but the Western-style toilet is becoming more prevalent and appears wherever foreign tourists can be found.

If you encounter a squat, here's what you should know. You should straddle the two foot pads and face the door. To flush use the plastic bowl to scoop water out of the adjacent

basin and pour into the toilet bowl. Some places supply a small pack of toilet paper at the entrance (5B), otherwise bring your own stash or wipe the old-fashioned way with water.

Even in places where sit-down toilets are installed, the septic system may not be designed to take toilet paper. In such cases there will be a waste basket where you're supposed to place used toilet paper and feminine hygiene products. Some toilets also come with a small spray hose – Thailand's version of the bidet.

Tourist Information

Tourism Authority of Thailand

(TAT; 📞 02 250 5500, nationwide 1672; www.tourismthailand.org; 1600 Th Phetchaburi; 🕐 8.30am-4.30pm; Ⓜ Phetchaburi exit 2) Government-operated tourist information and promotion service founded in 1960. Produces excellent pamphlets on sightseeing; check the website for contact information.

Travellers with Disabilities

Thailand presents one large, ongoing obstacle course for the mobility impaired. With its high kerbs, uneven footpaths and nonstop traffic, Thai cities can be particularly difficult. In Bangkok many streets must be crossed on pedestrian bridges flanked with steep stairways, while buses and boats don't stop long enough even for the fully abled. Rarely are there any ramps or other access points for wheelchairs.

A number of more expensive top-end hotels make consistent design efforts to provide disabled access to their properties. Other deluxe hotels with high employee-to-guest ratios are better equipped to accommodate the mobility impaired by providing staff help where building design fails. For the rest, you're pretty much left to your own resources.

Download Lonely Planet's free Accessible Travel guide from http://lptravel.to/AccessibleTravel. Alternatively, some organisations that offer tips on international travel include the following:

Accessible Journeys (www.disabilitytravel.com)

Asia Pacific Development Centre on Disability (www.apcdfoundation.org)

Mobility International USA (www.miusa.org)

Society for Accessible Travel & Hospitality (www.sath.org)

Wheelchair Holidays @ Thailand (www.wheelchairtours.com)

Visas

○ Most nationalities can receive a 30-day visa exemption on arrival at international airports or a 15-day visa at land borders; a 60-day tourist visa is available through Thai consulates.

○ Thailand's **Ministry of Foreign Affairs** (📞 02 203 5000; www.mfa.go.th) oversees immigration and visa issues. In the past several years there have been new rules almost annually regarding visas and extensions; the best online monitor is Thaivisa (www.thaivisa.com).

○ Citizens of 62 countries (including most European countries, Australia, New Zealand and the USA) can enter Thailand at no charge. Depending on nationality, these citizens are issued a 14- to 90-day visa exemption if they arrive by air (most nationalities receive 30 days) or for 15 to 30 days by land.

Language

In Thai the meaning of a single syllable may be altered by means of different tones. Standard Thai has five tones: low (eg *bàht*), mid (eg *dee*), falling (eg *mâi*), high (eg *máh*) and rising (eg *săhm*). The range of all five tones is relative to each speaker's vocal range, so there is no fixed 'pitch' intrinsic to the language.

Read our pronunciation guides as if they were English and you'll be understood. The hyphens indicate syllable breaks; some syllables are further divided with a dot to help you pronounce compound vowels (eg *mêu·a-rai*). Note that **b** is a hard 'p' sound, almost like a 'b' (eg in 'hip-bag'); **d** is a hard 't' sound, like a sharp 'd' (eg in 'mid-tone'); **ng** is pronounced as in 'singing', but in Thai it can also occur at the start of a word; and **r** is pronounced as in 'run' but flapped, and in everyday speech it's often pronounced like 'l'.

To enhance your trip with a phrasebook, visit **lonelyplanet. com**. Lonely Planet iPhone phrasebooks are available through the Apple App store.

Basics

Hello.	สวัสดี	*sà-wàt-dee*
Goodbye.	ลาก่อน	*lah gòrn*
Yes./No.	ใช่/ไม่	*châi/mâi*
Please.	ขอ	*kŏr*
Thank you.	ขอบคุณ	*kòrp kun*

You're welcome.	ยินดี	*yin dee*
Excuse me.	ขออภัย	*kŏr à-pai*
Sorry.	ขอโทษ	*kŏr tôht*

How are you?
สบายดีไหม *sà-bai dee măi*

Fine. And you?
สบายดีครับ/ค่ำ *sà-bai dee kráp/*
แล้วคุณล่ะ *kâ láa·ou kun lâ* (m/f)

Do you speak English?
คุณพูดภาษา *kun pôot pah-săh*
อังกฤษได้ไหม *ang-grìt dâi măi*

I don't understand.
ผม/ดิฉัน ไม่ *pŏm/dì-chăn mâi*
เข้าใจ *kôw jai* (m/f)

Eating & Drinking

I'd like (the menu), please.
ขอ (รายการ *kŏr (rai gahn*
อาหาร) หน่อย *ah-hăhn) nòy*

I don't eat ...
ผม/ดิฉัน *pŏm/dì-chăn*
ไม่กิน ... *mâi gin ...* (m/f)

eggs	ไข่	*kài*
fish	ปลา	*blah*
red meat	เนื้อแดง	*néu·a daang*
nuts	ถั่ว	*tòo·a*

That was delicious!
อร่อยมาก *à-ròy mâhk*

Cheers!
ไชโย — *chai-yoh*

Please bring the bill.
ขอบิลหน่อย — *kŏr bin nòy*

cafe	ร้านกาแฟ	*ráhn gah-faa*
market	ตลาด	*đà-làht*
restaurant	ร้านอาหาร	*ráhn ah-hăhn*
vegetarian	เจ	*jair*

Meat & Fish

beef	เนื้อ	*néu·a*
chicken	ไก่	*gài*
crab	ปู	*boo*
duck	เป็ด	*bèt*
fish	ปลา	*blah*
meat	เนื้อ	*néu·a*
pork	หมู	*mŏo*
squid	ปลาหมึก	*blah mèuk*
seafood	อาหารทะเล	*ah-hăhn tá-lair*

Fruit & Vegetables

banana	กล้วย	*glôo·ay*
beans	ถั่ว	*tòo·a*
coconut	มะพร้าว	*má-prów*
eggplant	มะเขือ	*má-kĕu·a*
fruit	ผลไม้	*pŏn-lá-mái*
guava	ฝรั่ง	*fa-ràng*
lime	มะนาว	*má-now*
mango	มะม่วง	*má-môo·ang*
mangosteen	มังคุด	*mang-kút*

mushrooms	เห็ด	*hèt*
nuts	ถั่ว	*tòo·a*
papaya	มะละกอ	*má-lá-gor*
potatoes	มันฝรั่ง	*man fa-ràng*
rambutan	เงาะ	*ngó*
tamarind	มะขาม	*má-kăhm*
tomatoes	มะเขือเทศ	*má-kĕu·a têt*
vegetables	ผัก	*pàk*
watermelon	แตงโม	*đaang moh*

Drinks

beer	เบียร์	*bee·a*
coffee	กาแฟ	*gah-faa*
milk	นมจืด	*nom jèut*
orange juice	น้ำส้ม	*nám sôm*
soy milk	น้ำเต้าหู้	*nám đôw hôo*
sugar-cane juice	น้ำอ้อย	*nám ôy*
tea	ชา	*chah*
water	น้ำดื่ม	*nám dèum*

Other

chilli	พริก	*prík*
egg	ไข่	*kài*
fish sauce	น้ำปลา	*nám blah*
noodles	เส้น	*sên*
pepper	พริกไทย	*prík tai*
rice	ข้าว	*kôw*
salad	ผักสด	*pàk sòt*
salt	เกลือ	*gleu·a*
soup	น้ำซุป	*nám súp*

soy sauce	น้ำซีอิ๊ว	nám see-éw
sugar	น้ำตาล	nám đahn
tofu	เต้าหู้	đôw hôo

Shopping

I'd like to buy ...
อยากจะซื้อ ...   yàhk jà séu ...

How much is it?
เท่าไร   tôw-rai

That's too expensive.
แพงไป   paang bai

Can you lower the price?
ลดราคาได้ไหม   lót rah-kah dâi măi

There's a mistake in the bill.
บิลใบนี้ผิด   bin bai née pìt ná
นะครับ/ค่ะ   kráp/kâ (m/f)

Emergencies

Help!	ช่วยด้วย	chôo·ay
		dôo·ay
Go away!	ไปให้พ้น	bai hâi pón

Call a doctor!
เรียกหมอหน่อย   rêe·ak mŏr nòy

Call the police!
เรียกตำรวจ   rêe·ak đam·ròo·at
หน่อย   nòy

I'm ill.
ผม/ดิฉัน   pŏm/dì·chăn
ป่วย   bòo·ay (m/f)

I'm lost.
ผม/ดิฉัน   pŏm/dì·chăn
หลงทาง   lŏng tahng (m/f)

Where are the toilets?
ห้องน้ำ   hôrng nám
อยู่ที่ไหน   yòo têe năi

Time, Days & Numbers

What time is it?
กี่โมงแล้ว   gèe mohng láa·ou

morning	เช้า	chów
afternoon	บ่าย	bài
evening	เย็น	yen

yesterday	เมื่อวาน	mêu·a wahn
today	วันนี้	wan née
tomorrow	พรุ่งนี้	prûng née

Monday	วันจันทร์	wan jan
Tuesday	วันอังคาร	wan ang-kahn
Wednesday	วันพุธ	wan pút
Thursday	วันพฤหัสฯ	wan pá-réu-hàt
Friday	วันศุกร์	wan sùk
Saturday	วันเสาร์	wan sŏw
Sunday	วันอาทิตย์	wan ah-tít

1	หนึ่ง	*nèung*
2	สอง	*sŏrng*
3	สาม	*săhm*
4	สี่	*sèe*
5	ห้า	*hâh*
6	หก	*hòk*
7	เจ็ด	*jèt*
8	แปด	*bàat*
9	เก้า	*gôw*
10	สิบ	*sìp*
20	ยี่สิบ	*yêe-sìp*
21	ยี่สิบเอ็ด	*yêe-sìp-èt*
30	สามสิบ	*săhm-sìp*
40	สี่สิบ	*sèe-sìp*
50	ห้าสิบ	*hâh-sìp*
60	หกสิบ	*hòk-sìp*
70	เจ็ดสิบ	*jèt-sìp*
80	แปดสิบ	*bàat-sìp*
90	เก้าสิบ	*gôw-sìp*
100	หนึ่งร้อย	*nèung róy*
1000	หนึ่งพัน	*nèung pan*
1,000,000	หนึ่งล้าน	*nèung láhn*

Transport & Directions

Where is ...?
... อยู่ที่ไหน   *... yòo têe năi*

What's the address?
ที่อยู่คืออะไร   *têe yòo keu à-rai*

Can you show me (on the map)?
ให้ดู (ในแผนที่)   *hâi doo (nai păn têe)*
ได้ไหม   *dâi măi*

Turn left/right.
เลี้ยวซ้าย/ขวา   *lée·o sái/kwăh*

bicycle rickshaw
สามล้อ   *săhm lór*

boat	เรือ	*reu·a*
bus	รถเมล์	*rót mair*
car	รถเก๋ง	*rót gĕng*

motorcycle
มอร์เตอร์ไซค์   *mor-deu-sai*

taxi
รถแท็กซี่   *rót táak·sêe*

plane	เครื่องบิน	*krêu·ang bin*
train	รถไฟ	*rót fai*
túk-túk	ตุ๊ก ๆ	*đúk đúk*

When's the first bus?
รถเมล์คันแรก   *rót mair kan râak*
มาเมื่อไร   *mah mêu·a rai*

A (one-way/return) ticket, please.
ขอตั๋ว (เที่ยว   *kŏr đŏo·a (têe·o*
เดียว/ไปกลับ).   *dee·o/bai glàp)*

What time does it get to ...?
ถึง ... กี่โมง   *tĕung ... gèe mohng*

Does it stop at ...?
รถจอดที่ ... ไหม   *rót jòrt têe ... măi*

I'd like to get off at ...
ขอลงที่ ...   *kŏr long têe ...*

Index

See also separate subindexes for:

⊗ **Eating p186**

⊙ **Drinking p187**

✪ **Entertainment p188**

🔒 **Shopping p188**

Sights **000**
Map Pages **000**

Behind the Scenes

Send Us Your Feedback

We love to hear from travellers – your comments help make our books better. We read every word, and we guarantee that your feedback goes straight to the authors. Visit **lonelyplanet.com/contact** to submit your updates and suggestions.

Note: We may edit, reproduce and incorporate your comments in Lonely Planet products such as guidebooks, websites and digital products, so let us know if you don't want your comments reproduced or your name acknowledged. For a copy of our privacy policy visit lonelyplanet.com/privacy.

Austin's Thanks

A big thanks to destination editors Dora Ball and Clifton Wilkinson, as well as to all the people on the ground in Bangkok.

Acknowledgements

Cover photograph: túk-túks in downtown Bangkok, Evgeny Tchebotarev/500px © Photographs pp26–7 (from left): Travelmania; Kriang Kan; Adumm 76/Shutterstock ©

This Book

This 6th edition of Lonely Planet's *Pocket Bangkok* guidebook was researched and written by Austin Bush, who also wrote the previous two editions. This guidebook was produced by the following:

Destination Editors
Tanya Parker, Dora Ball, Clifton Wilkinson

Series Designer
Campbell McKenzie

Cartographic Series Designer
Wayne Murphy

Senior Product Editor
Kate Chapman

Product Editor
Rachel Rawling

Senior Cartographer
Diana von Holdt

Book Designer
Virginia Moreno

Cartographer
Julie Sheridan

Assisting Editors Judith Bamber, Imogen Bannister, Melanie Dankel, Andrea Dobbin, Jennifer Hattam, Gabrielle Innes, Rosie Nicholson, Lou McGregor, Tamara Sheward, Maja Vatrić

Cover Researchers
Brendan Dempsey-Spencer, Naomi Parker

Thanks to Nicolas P Combremont, Ruth Cosgrove, Laura Crawford, Bruce Evans, Blaze Hadzik, James Hardy, Liz Heynes, Simon Hoskins, Chris Lee Ack, Jean-Pierre Masclef, Anne Mason, Liam McGrellis, Harshvardhan Modak, Dan Moore, Darren O'Connell, Martine Power, Kirsten Rawlings, Kathryn Rowan, Wibowo Rusli, Dianne Schallmeiner, Ellie Simpson, John Taufa, Angela Tinson, Juan Winata

Our Writer

Austin Bush

Austin Bush came to Thailand in 1999 as part of a language study programme hosted by Chiang Mai University. The lure of city life, employment and spicy food eventually led Austin to Bangkok. City employment and spicy food have managed to keep him there ever since. These days, Austin works as a writer and photographer, and in addition to having contributed to numerous books, magazines and websites, has contributed text and photos to more than 20 Lonely Planet titles including *Bangkok; The Food Book; Food Lover's Guide to the World; Laos; Malaysia, Singapore & Brunei; Myanmar (Burma); Thailand; Thailand's Islands & Beaches; Vietnam, Cambodia, Laos & Northern Thailand;* and *The World's Best Street Food.*

Published by Lonely Planet Global Limited
CRN 554153
6th edition – Oct 2018
ISBN 978 1 78657 533 3
© Lonely Planet 2018   Photographs © as indicated 2018
10 9 8 7 6 5 4 3 2 1
Printed in Malaysia